T0333992

The Textile Industry and Exports in Post-Liberalization India

This book is a comprehensive examination of the Indian textile industry and the various determinants affecting its export performance, trends in labour, and capital productivity in the post-liberalization years. Employing 45 million people, including skilled and unskilled workers, the Indian textile and clothing industry occupies a significant position in the Indian economy in terms of industrial production, employment, and exports.

This work traces the growth and expansion of this industry in the post-reform period and studies its contributions to the economic development of the nation. It discusses global trade agreements, India's share in international exports, and its major trading partners across the globe including the USA, UK, UAE, Germany, and China. It also provides recommendations to Indian policy makers for a possible improvement in the textile exports across the globe.

The Textile Industry and Exports in Post-Liberalization India will be of interest to students and researchers of politics and international relations, economics, development studies, labour economics, sociology and social policy, and South Asian studies.

Rahul Dhiman is Assistant Professor at the Department of Business Management, Dr. Y.S. Parmar University of Horticulture and Forestry, a State University of Himachal Pradesh, India. He has published extensively in Scopus- and ABDC-listed international journals.

Manoj Sharma is Assistant Professor at the Department of Humanities and Social Sciences, National Institute of Technology, Hamirpur, Himachal Pradesh, India. His research interests include international business, applied economics, environmental economics and transportation management. He has published extensively in national and international journals.

The Textile Industry and Exports in Post-Liberalization India

Rahul Dhiman and Manoj Sharma

Routledge
Taylor & Francis Group

LONDON AND NEW YORK

First published 2021
by Routledge
2 Park Square, Milton Park, Abingdon, Oxon OX14 4RN

and by Routledge
52 Vanderbilt Avenue, New York, NY 10017

Routledge is an imprint of the Taylor & Francis Group, an informa business

British Library Cataloguing-in-Publication Data
A catalogue record for this book is available from the British Library

Library of Congress Cataloging-in-Publication Data
Names: Dhiman, Rahul, author.
Title: Textile industry and exports in post liberalization India / Rahul Dhiman.
Description: New York, NY : Routledge, 2020. | Includes bibliographical references and index.
Identifiers: LCCN 2020005599 (print) | LCCN 2020005600 (ebook)
Subjects: LCSH: Textile industry—India. | Clothing trade—India.
Classification: LCC HD9866.I42 D45 2020 (print) | LCC HD9866.I42 (ebook) | DDC 338.4/767700954—dc23
LC record available at https://lccn.loc.gov/2020005599
LC ebook record available at https://lccn.loc.gov/2020005600

ISBN: 978-1-138-34724-3 (hbk)
ISBN: 978-0-367-50482-3 (pbk)
ISBN: 978-1-003-05029-2 (ebk)

Typeset in Sabon
by Apex CoVantage, LLC

Contents

Figures

Note: Figures No. 4.1 to 4.6; 4.7 to 4.12 and 4.13 to 4.18 are for Textile Industry, 'Textiles' group and 'Textile Products' group, respectively.

Tables

Preface

This book serves to consolidate the knowledge that has been acquired from being an academician and researcher of the Indian textile industry. It is our aim, in examining the export performance, trends in the labour and capital productivity, direction of various textile commodities, and the key determinants that affect the export competitiveness that recommendations be provided to the policy makers. The author also aims to share research outputs that promote best practices in and improve the export competitiveness of the Indian textile industry.

The book is organized in five chapters. **Chapter 1—An introductory note about the Indian textile and clothing industry** provides historical overview, the growth of the textile industry and various agreements such as MFA and ATC. The contribution of industry in economy, share in world textile exports, and in total Indian exports and major issues of the industry are discussed in this chapter.

Chapter 2—Conceptual outline operationally defines the determinants of export competitiveness by understanding various definitions, models, and theories specified by the scientists, management thinkers, and scholars. The interrelationships among the variables and various theories are also discussed in this chapter.

Chapter 3—Export performance and direction of textile exports presents the growth, export performance, and direction of Indian textile exports and its two groups, namely the 'Textiles' and 'Textile Products' groups.

Chapter 4—Determinants of export competitiveness highlights the empirical findings of the impact of select determinants on the export competitiveness. Empirical findings are based on various tools and techniques as suggested by previous studies.

Chapter 5—A summing up and policy implications summarizes the work carried out in the present book. The main contributions and policy implications on the basis of the results are presented in this chapter.

This book consolidates selected research findings of significance and relevance to the practitioners of textile firms from the author's scholarly endeavours as an educator and researcher in the field. The author hopes that the reader will find this book interesting and informative about the latest developments in the Indian textile exports. This book focuses on the performance of Indian textile commodities at both aggregate and disaggregate levels. The major Unique Selling Propositions of the book are as follows:

- State-of-the-art and detailed coverage of the textile commodities at HS two- and HS four-digit level.
- Coverage of the various productivity measures such as labour and capital productivity and its impact on the export competitiveness.
- Latest methodologies used to analyse the impact of selected determinants on the export competitiveness.
- Strong and well-balanced combination of key performing and non-performing textile commodities.
- Recommendations to the policy makers so that the performance of textile exports across the globe can be increased.

The volume addresses a number of arguments, which are as follows:

- How has the textile industry grown in the post-reform period?
- What are the labour and capital productivity trends in the industry?
- How have the textile commodities performed in the global markets?
- Has the industry been able to acquire new export destinations?
- Which are the key determinants that impact the export competitiveness of the industry?

Hence the volume examines the export performance, trends in the labour and capital productivity, direction of various textile commodities, and the key determinants that affect the export competitiveness so that the recommendations can be provided to the policy makers.

Rahul Dhiman and Manoj Sharma

Acknowledgements

This book has been far too long in the making. In the course, I have accumulated many debts and obligations, which are too numerous to list and which I can never adequately repay. In completing this volume, I received support from many people. First, I sincerely thank my elder brother, Dr Rohit Dhiman, for his cooperation and inspiration without which it would not have been possible for me to complete this volume. It is my pleasure and privilege to offer thanks and gratitude to my parents, who always encouraged me and stayed by my side whenever I needed them. I also acknowledge with utmost affection the unending support, immense understanding, and everlasting love of my wife Shilpa and loving daughter Sanvi.

Rahul Dhiman

Abbreviations

ATC	Agreement on Textile and Clothing
ASI	Annual Survey of Industries
ADF	Augmented Dickey-Fuller
AIC	Akaike Information Criterion
CP	capital productivity
CAGR	compound annual growth rate
CMS	constant market share
CSO	Central Statistical Organization
DGCI&S	Directorate General of Commercial Intelligence and Statistics
DV	dependent variable
DIF	difference
D	difference
DSB	Dispute Settlement Body
EU	European Union
ECA	Essential Commodities Act
EXIM	export import
ER	exchange rate
EEC	European Economic Community
EPWRF	Economic and Political Weekly Research Foundation
EC	export competitiveness
GVA	gross value added
GDP	gross domestic product
GATT	General Agreement on Tariffs and Trade
GFCF	gross fixed capital formation
H-O	Heckscher-Ohlin
HS	harmonized system
IMF	International Monetary Fund
JB	Jarque–Bera
LP	labour productivity
MFA	Multi-Fiber Agreement
NTP	New Textiles Policy
NBER	National Bureau of Economic Research

NA	North America
NEER	nominal effective exchange rate
NPC	National Productivity Council
NIC	National Industrial Classification
OLS	ordinary least square
PMS	performance management system
REER	real effective exchange rate
RBI	Reserve Bank of India
RMG	readymade garments
R&D	research and development
SSI	small-scale industry
SAARC	South Asian Association for Regional Cooperation
SC	Schwarz Information Criterion
SIP	Statement of Industrial Policy
TUFS	Technology Upgradation Fund Scheme
TMB	Textiles Monitoring Body
TEXPROCIL	The Cotton Textile Export Promotion Council
TFP	total factor productivity
ULC	unit labour cost
UAE	United Arab Emirates
USA	United States of America
USD	United States dollar
UN	United Nations
VECM	vector error correction model
VAR	vector autoregression
WTO	World Trade Organization
WITS	World Integrated Trade Solution

1 An introductory note about the Indian textile and clothing industry

Introduction

The Indian textile and clothing industry is one of the largest industries of modern India and also the largest foreign-exchange-earner of the nation. The introductory chapter of this volume deals with historical overview of the Indian textile industry, key agreements and policies, contribution of the textile industry in economic development, and major issues of industry. This volume shall make an effort to address export performance, direction, and various determinants affecting the export performance of the Indian textile industry in the following chapters.

The textile and apparel industry in India enjoys a rich heritage, as it was the well-organized industry that came up in India first. A country like India which has abundant availability of raw materials has always been recognized for textile goods since very ancient times. The textile industry is among the leading sectors that have been regarded as the route to the industrial development by many nations across the world. This industry has the power to transform a country from poverty to prosperity provided continuous steps are undertaken by the government. This sector has played a crucial part in achieving high economic growth, offering employment opportunities, growth in industrial production, and bringing foreign exchange reserves. The textile industry also contributes to the total export basket. The commencement of globalization of trade and economic liberalization in India posed new challenges as well as opportunities for the textile firms in India. The economic reforms since 1991 have brought a new regime for the textile and clothing sector, and much-needed action plans were undertaken to boost the exports. The reforms identified the major role of the textile industry to ensure growth in apparel manufacturing of satisfactory quality at realistic prices in order to meet the clothing needs of increasing people. The policy reforms visualized that this crucial aim could be achieved through efficiencies in the cost and free participation of market forces.

Historical overview of the Indian textile industry

The products of the textile industry are utilized by everyone. The process of the textile industry starts from the stage of manufacturing raw materials to the manufacture of a broad range of semi-finished as well as finished products. The raw material of the industry comprises natural and man-made fibres. In the period before colonization, the manually operated textile machines of India were among the best across the globe and served as replicas of the manufacture of the textile machines in Britain and Germany (Roy, 1996). The Indian textile industry had gone through tough times during the colonial regime. However, the industry was revived in the 19th century, when the first textile mill in the nation was introduced in Calcutta near Fort Gloster in 1818. The development of the textile industry in the country started gaining momentum due to the accessibility of home-grown cotton and British machinery. The textile commodities were very competitive during this period, and the British knew that they were unable to compete with it. Tariffs were designed in such a manner that the British goods would go through the Indian market almost free of cost. However, the products of India were kept out of the market of Britain. This arrangement stayed in place until the fight for independence began in India. The major activities related to the textile and clothing industry are outlined as mentioned below:

- The management of raw materials, i.e. manufacturing fibres like cotton, flax, silk, wool, jute, etc. Man-made fibres comprise a variety of textile fibres and production of yarns through spinning. The natural cellulosic fibres, synthetic fibres, and fibres from inorganic materials such as carbon, glass, and metal.
- The activities related to knitting and weaving.
- The finishing actions for the purpose of providing fabrics the visual and physical properties to meet the demands of consumers such as bleaching, printing, dyeing, impregnating, etc.
- The last activity converts these fabrics into finished products, such as clothing products, carpets and other textile floor coverings, common household textile products such as kitchen linen, bed linen, toilet linen, curtains, etc.

The textile sector of India can broadly be categorized as (i) organized mill sector and (ii) unorganized decentralized sector. The organized mill sector comprises an updated and highly mechanized mill sector. Spinning mill and composite mill are two types of such mills. A composite mill is a place where the activities of spinning, weaving, and processing are performed under one roof. The decentralized mill sector has insufficient organizational setup in terms of updated technology or machinery requirements, production pattern, employment, etc. The unorganized mill sector is occupied primarily in performing activity related to weaving. As a result, it gets a great deal reliant on the organized mill in order to meet the need of yarn. The weaving segment is identified as one of the segments where lack of technology is found in the entire system. The decentralized mill sector comprises three prime segments such as powerloom, handloom, and hosiery.

The Indian textile and clothing value chain comprises four major stages, namely ginning and spinning, weaving and knitting, processing, and clothing manufacturing. The process of spinning includes the conversion of cotton or manmade fiber into yarn. In the case of cotton, before spinning, ginning is done to remove the seeds and impurities. Then cotton or manmade yarn is converted into woven or knitted fabrics. Processing includes bleaching, dyeing, and printing, which delivers finished fabric to be used for the production of clothes. The manufacturing of clothes is the final stage in which the activities related to cutting, stitching, designing, finishing, and packaging are completed for supply in the market.

The textile industry passed through the stages of growth and depression. The cotton textile industry continuously grew in the second half of the 19th century. One hundred seventy-eight cotton textile mills were present by the end of the century. The industry was again in depression from 1922 to 1937. However, the Second World War, during which textile import from Japan completely stopped, brought about an unparalleled expansion of this industry. The number of mills grew from 178 to 249 in the year 1921, and 417 mills were present by the year 1945, offering employment to 5.10 lakh workers (Sastry, 1984). India's apparel exports are made largely of cotton because of the easy accessibility of cotton fabrics at globally economical prices. The export of cotton grew from US$1107 million in 1991 to US$7508 million in the year 2015 (United Nations Comtrade Database, 2016). The most important cotton-producing states are Gujarat, Maharashtra, Punjab, and Andhra Pradesh. Punjab generates around 70 percent of the high-quality cotton in India.

Silk is the dominating fiber used in the Indian textile industry. The second-largest manufacturer of silk in the world is India, contributing about 18 percent to the global production (EXIM, 2008). Silk exports performed well in the period from 1991 to 2015, and exports grew from US$128.4 million in 1991 to US$335.2 million in the year 2010. Thereafter, a huge downfall can be observed, and it decreased to US$111.2 million in 2015 (United Nations Comtrade Database, 2016). Apart from cotton and silk, India is the largest manufacturer and consumer of raw jute across the globe and is the seventh-largest manufacturer of raw wool. Although the woollen textile and clothing industry is reasonably small as compared to the cotton and man-made fiber-based textiles and clothing industry, the woollen sector plays a significant role, as it links the rural sector with the textile-manufacturing sector.

Key agreements in textile and clothing

The first Multi-Fiber Agreement (MFA) was agreed in 1973 under American support and was put into practice from 1 January 1974. MFA-I was a tool of agreement intended to deal with textile trade to facilitate those nations that have lost competitiveness in the world trade. MFA-I was followed by MFA-II, which was implemented on January 1, 1978 as a consequence of a set of rules which was signed on December 14, 1977 and was extended for four years. MFA-II also focussed upon liberalization in the industry with GATT regulations. MFA came back as MFA-III in January 1982. The third MFA (1982–1986) was discussed in an environment of growing issues among developing nations about the undesirable influence on their exports earlier. The fourth MFA continued to have some unwanted features, and its tenure was extended to 1991. In the Uruguay Round of trade negotiations in 1994, it was decided that MFA would be phased out in stages through the introduction of the ATC. As a result, the Agreement on Textile and Clothing (ATC) took over MFA. The MFA was fully phased out on 1 January 2005. The abolition of the quota era was regarded as both an opportunity and a threat. It was an opportunity since the marketplace would no longer be limited and a threat because markets would no longer be assured by quotas (Kathuria and Bharadwaj, 1998; Verma, 2002). The issues of developing countries were addressed in the ATC. The ATC included various levels for abolishing the quantitative barriers in the commencement of 1995, 1998, 2002, and 2005. The ATC provided a comprehensive catalog of goods to which it is applied. The list was on the basis of harmonized system (HS) description and coding system nomenclature. The Textiles Monitoring Body (TMB) and Dispute Settlement Body were introduced in order to administer the functioning of ATC, regularly inspect all methods under this agreement, and settle disputes.

Key policies

Textile policy in 1985 was designed with an objective to facilitate the industry to raise manufacturing of superior-value clothing at realistic prices for the huge population of the nation and for the purpose of export. During this time, textiles were under the Essential Commodities Act, in which rivalry and market dynamics were unfamiliar. The government kept coming with continuous changes in this policy as per market forces.

The aggressive policy that commenced for the Indian textile industry was the introduction of the National Textile Policy (NTP) in 2000. The broad objective was to ensure an increase in the foreign exchange earnings, and it included logical forecasting for expansion of all the segments involved with the textile industry. The vital target finalized in the textile policy was to move forward the worth of textile and clothing exports from US$11 billion to US$50 billion by 2010 with the contribution of clothing at US$25 billion.

The government of India made an expert committee to check the NTP, 2000, and create the NTP, 2013. The NTP, 2000, was formulated 13 years before, and since then, the business has undergone a number of changes on the home and global fronts. The textile industry of India witnessed modernization and technological advancement in the previous decade. The export quota era had been abolished in 2004 in the international trade scenario. The new developments in the worldwide textile industry present massive opportunities for the industry to add to its contribution in global trade with a framework of helpful guiding principles. For this reason, the government aimed to put together a fresh superior textile policy to deal with issues of skilled labour and labour reforms and capture investments in the textile segment to show a way for the industry. The new NTP, 2013, was formulated for offering a potential road map for the entire industry. This road map had the provision of 3 percent interest subvention, addition of fresh markets like New Zealand, Latvia, Lithuania, and Bulgaria under the Focus market scheme, and an incremental export incentive plan. Exporters are motivated to discover fresh markets such as Latin America, Australia, Japan, Africa, Israel, Southeast Asia, and the Middle East to decrease reliance on Western markets. In addition to this, the Indian government also approved numerous rebates and incentives to the textile and clothing industry as a consequence of a substantial rise in total production of this industry.

Indian textile exports and their contribution to the economy

The introduction of economic reforms gave a boost to the textile industry of India. The boundaries are not limited now, and barriers to international trade are abolished so that free trade among countries can take place. Many developed countries have economically gained a lot from their exports after the elimination of quota systems and liberal policies. The export segment is well thought-out as a driving force for speeding up the course of economic growth. Traditionally, textiles have emerged as a significant element of India's export. The raw material availability in abundance, cheap labour cost, and thriving domestic market are the main strengths of the Indian textile industry. This, as a result, provided recognition to the textile industry in the industrial map of the nation. Due to the huge size and early progress of the Indian textile industry, it was expected for India to begin as an exporter of textile items in the initial phases. The apparel manufactured in India is exported to more than 120 countries. The markets of the USA and EU account for 76 percent of the total exports. Textile exports of India increased significantly from US$4865.3 million in 1991 to US$37162 million in 2015. The contribution of India to the world exports of textile and clothing in the past has been small, but it started to grow considerably after 1991, reaching 2.02 percent of global exports in 1991 and 4.99 percent in 2015 (see Table 1.1). The growth in terms of number of factories, gross value added (GVA), and capital stock in the post-reform regime is shown in Figure 1.1.

But still, this cannot be regarded as a significant improvement due to the fact that the industry has a number of strengths like raw material availability and cheap labour. However, the percentage contribution of textile exports in total exports has declined continuously from 25.5 percent in 1991 to

Table 1.1 India's Share in World Textile Exports

Year	Textile Exports (US$ Million)		India's Share in World Textile Exports (%)
	World	India	
1991	226085	4565	2.02
1992	249301	5678	2.28
1993	242244	5711	2.36
1994	272340	7179	2.64
1995	310672	8098	2.61
1996	318821	9158	2.87
1997	333355	9381	2.81
1998	335794	9008	2.68
1999	330842	9981	3.02
2000	352813	11151	3.16
2001	342375	10600	3.10
2002	358295	11360	3.17
2003	406206	12490	3.07
2004	454886	14155	3.11
2005	481866	17034	3.54
2006	529239	19102	3.61
2007	587250	20974	3.57
2008	613901	22702	3.70
2009	528367	21913	4.15
2010	606289	27128	4.47
2011	712367	33374	4.68
2012	704984	32683	4.64
2013	765508	40193	5.25
2014	803789	38597	4.80
2015	744413	37162	4.99

Source: UN Comtrade Database.

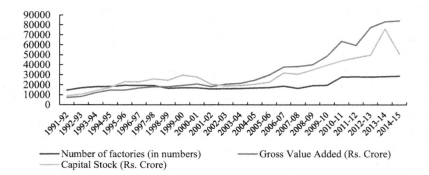

Number of factories (in numbers)   Gross Value Added (Rs. Crore)
Capital Stock (Rs. Crore)

Figure 1.1 Growth Rate of Indian Textile Industry

Source: Annual Survey of Industries, various issues.

14.05 percent in 2015 (see Table 1.2). This can be attributed to the fact that the commodities other than textiles have also shown remarkable growth in the world market. The contribution of industry in the global exports of textile and apparel is still relatively low as compared to other countries, such as Singapore, South Korea, China, and Hong Kong.

The textile industry has a significant contribution in the export earnings and offers job opportunities to skilled and unskilled workers. It occupies a significant position in the Indian economy in terms of industrial production, employment, and exports and contributes to 10 percent of industrial production and 2 percent of gross domestic product (GDP). It employs 45 million people (second largest after agriculture) and supplies 13 percent of the country's export earnings (Ministry of Textiles, 2016–17).

The textile industry has played a vital role in the economic development of the developed nations. Nations such as Japan, Britain, Korea, and Taiwan have relied on textile and clothing exports for economic development.

Table 1.2 Share of India's Textile Exports in Its Total Exports

Year	Total Exports Total Textile		India's Share in World Textile Exports (%)
	(US$M)	(US$M)	
1991	17900	4565	25.5
1992	20711	5678	27.4
1993	22237	5711	25.7
1994	26330	7179	27.3
1995	31699	8098	25.5
1996	33468	9158	27.4
1997	34794	9381	27.0
1998	33207	9008	27.1
1999	36672	9981	27.2
2000	42358	11151	26.3
2001	43879	10600	24.2
2002	50098	11360	22.7
2003	59360	12490	21.0
2004	75904	14155	18.6
2005	100352	17034	17.0
2006	121200	19102	15.8
2007	145898	20974	14.4
2008	181860	22702	12.5
2009	176765	21913	12.4
2010	220408	27128	12.3
2011	301483	33374	11.1
2012	289564	32683	11.3
2013	336611	40193	11.9
2014	317544	38597	12.2
2015	264381	37162	14.0

Source: Same as in Table 1.1.

For example, textile and clothing exports jointly amount to 86 percent of Bangladesh's total exports. This ratio is 80 percent for Cambodia, 73 percent for Pakistan, 58 percent for Mauritius, and 57 percent for Sri Lanka. Nations such as Turkey and Bulgaria are reliant on textile and clothing exports in Europe (USITC, 2001). This reveals that the textile industry has not only contributed to the progress of India, but several other nations have also witnessed economic development due to the textile exports.

Indian textile exports are diversified across the globe and have found new destinations following the pulling out of MFA and the decline in duties. Indian textile exports are primarily directed to South Asian countries and the South Asian Association for Regional Cooperation (SAARC) nations. The USA still remained the major market for exports in the year 2015, with the highest share of 19.08 percent. However, the share declined in comparison to 1995 and 2005, followed by UAE (9.84 percent share), UK (6.96 percent), Sri Lanka (5.36 percent share), and Germany (4.39 percent), which indicates addition of more export destinations for Indian textile exports (UN Comtrade Database, 2016). This reveals that Indian textile commodities have been able to acquire new export markets in the global market. Hence, it can be concluded that India's textile exports are diversified to a number of international markets in the post-reform period. From the earlier discussion, it is clear that the textile industry is backbone of the economy, as it contributes to the economic development of the nation, industrial production, and total export basket. The numerous controls that were imposed in the pre-reform regime were relaxed in the post-reform era in terms of various textile policies, quota elimination, etc. As a result, India's share in world textile exports improved from 2.02 percent in 1991 to 4.90 percent in 2015. Indian textile commodities have found new destinations in the international market, and the two prime export partners of India are the USA and EU. However, an interesting fact that comes up is that the percentage contribution of textile exports in total exports has declined continuously from 25.5 percent in 1991 to 14.05 percent in 2015. So it would be interesting to examine the textile export performance at both aggregate and disaggregate levels in the post-reform regime and the factors influencing the export competitiveness (EC).

Major issues of the textile industry

The objectives of the economic reforms were to speed up economic development and to achieve higher growth in productivity. It has been argued that opening up of the economy will show the way to better growth and upgrade the productivity levels. However, the post-liberalization regime did not facilitate raising manufacturing and productivity in the textile industry as desired. The previous studies of Goldar (2000), Balakrishnan and Babu (2003), and Kannan and Raveendran (2009) also established a decline in growth and productivity trends during the post-reform regime.

It can be noted that the share of the Indian textile and clothing industry, in spite of being the largest foreign-exchange-earning industrial sector, the global textile and clothing exports is still relatively low as compared to other Asian countries such as Singapore, China, South Korea, and Hong Kong. The share of India in world textile exports has not improved a great deal in the post-reform era despite the number of strengths that the Indian textile industry carries. The contribution of India's textile exports in total exports was 28 percent in 1991, which declined to 13 percent in 2015. So there is a need to examine the variables which are responsible for this kind of a trend, and weak as well as key textile commodities also need to be identified so that action plans can be formulated and export performance can be increased, which is the purpose of the book.

In addition to this, key determinants which affect the textile export performance also need to be examined carefully. India, in spite of having lower labour wage rates in comparison to China, has not been able to achieve the two-digit figure. This captures a lot of attention. There is need to examine the export performance and key determinants of the Indian textile industry at both aggregate and disaggregate levels in the post-reform regime (Dhiman and Sharma, 2016). Hence this book is a step in this direction and attempts to examine the performance of Indian textile exports at HS two- and HS four-digit levels and also examines the key determinants affecting the EC.

Why study determinants of export competitiveness?

There have been a large number of studies that investigate the relationship between exports and productivity. For example, studies by Bernard and Jensen (1998, 1999) on the United States; Aw, Chung, and Roberts (1998) on Taiwan and Korea; Clerides, Lach, and Tybout (1998) on Colombia, Mexico, and Morocco; Kraay (1999) on China; Wagner (2002) on Germany; Girma, Greenaway, and Kneller (2003) on the UK; and Dhiman and Sharma (2017a, 2017b, 2019) on India have all examined the exports–productivity linkage. However, all of these studies have not clearly investigated the factors responsible for the EC, especially in the Indian context. A few studies have also been conducted on the Indian textile industry at aggregate levels. However, there are significant analytical gaps at the disaggregate level that need to be addressed. Another study by Brown and Dev (1999) highlighted that important variables like labour and capital have not been studied, which are strongly related to the productivity trends. So in the light of these facts, it becomes very important to study the key determinants of export EC of the textile industry. The literature emphasizes exchange rate (ER), labour productivity (LP), capital productivity (CP), and unit labour cost (ULC) as the critical determinants of competitiveness and suggests the importance of these variables to sustain in the global competitive market. Another important determinant of EC chosen in this study is LP, since the industry is labour intensive. The growth in LP results in an increase in

EC. The ER is another determinant identified, and the previous study also indicates the need to identify the relationship between EC and exchange rate, as this relationship has not been comprehensively examined at the industry level (Ito and Shimizu, 2015). The variations in the exchange rate result in fluctuations in the demand for textile exports. The depreciation of currency made textile products cheaper. As a result, the demand for the product increases, which further led to a rise in exports. The literature also highlights labour cost as another determinant affecting the textile exports among Asian developing countries. The increase in labour costs gives rise to poor export performance. So minimizing ULC is a challenge being faced by the industries and the need of hour is to reduce the labour cost for the efficient working of the business enterprise.

The present book makes an effort to examine these variables in the post-reform era. In addition to this, some other important parameters such as growth trends in terms of GVA, the number of factories, the number of employees, and capital stock also need to be examined in order to access the Indian textile industry. Most of the studies analysed India's export performance at HS two-digit level. The present book is unique in the sense that it examines the performance of India's textile exports at HS two-digit and four-digit levels, involving a total of 149 products (see appendix), and also suggests measures to improve India's EC in textiles and clothing in the post-reform regime.

References

Aw, B., Chung, S., and Roberts, M. (1998). *Productivity and the decision to export market: Micro evidence from Taiwan and South Korea.* National Bureau of Economic Research, Working Paper, 6558.

Balakrishnan, P., and Babu, S. (2003). Growth and distribution in Indian industry in the nineties. *Economic & Political Weekly, 38*(38), 3997–4005.

Bernard, A. B., and Jensen, J. B. (1998). Exporters, jobs and wages in U.S. manufacturing, 1976–1987. *The Brooking Papers on Economic Activity: Microeconomics,* 67–119.

Bernard, A. B., and Jensen, J. B. (1999). Exceptional exporter performance: Cause, effect, or both. *Journal of International Economics, 47*(1), 1–25.

Brown, J. R., and Dev, C. S. (1999). Looking beyond RevPAR: Productivity consequences of hotel strategies. *The Cornell Hotel and Restaurant Administration Quarterly, 40*(2), 23–33.

Clerides, S. K., Lach, S., and Tybout, J. R. (1998). Is learning-by-exporting important? Micro dynamic evidence from Colombia, Mexico, and Morocco. *The Quarterly Journal of Economics, 113*(3), 903–947.

Dhiman, R., and Sharma, M. (2016). Examining the growth trends, direction and competitiveness of Indian textile exports in global trade. In A.K. Sinha, A. Pandey, A. K. Mohapatra, and S. Rana (Eds.), *Advances in management* (pp.193–200). New Delhi: Bloomsbury Publishing.

Dhiman, R., and Sharma, M. (2017a). Export competitiveness of Indian textile industry: Revealed comparative advantage analysis. *International Journal of Applied Business and Economic Research, 15*(9), 295–305.

Dhiman, R., and Sharma, M. (2017b). Productivity trends and determinants of Indian textile industry: A disaggregated analysis. *International Journal of Applied Business and Economic Research, 15*(22), 113–124.

Dhiman, R., and Sharma, M. (2019). Relation between labour productivity and export competitiveness of Indian textile industry: Cointegration and causality approach. *Vision: The Journal of Business Perspective, 23*(1), 22–30.

EXIM. (2008). *Indian textiles and clothing industry in global context: Salient features and issues.* Export Import Bank of India, Research Brief, 43.

Girma, S., Greenaway, D., and Kneller, R. (2003). Export market exit and performance dynamics: A causality analysis of matched firms. *Economics Letters, 80*(2), 181–187.

Goldar, B. (2000). Indian manufacturing: Productivity trends in pre and post-reform periods. *Economic & Political Weekly, 39*(46), 5033–5043.

Government of India. (1991–2017). *Annual survey of industries.* Retrieved from www.csoisw.gov.in/cms/En/1023-annual-survey-of-industries.aspx

Ito, K., and Shimizu, J. (2015). Industry-level competitiveness, productivity and effective exchange rates in East Asia. *Asian Economic Journal, 29*(2), 181–214.

Kannan, K. P., and Raveendran, G. (2009). Growth sans employment: A quarter century of jobless growth in India's organised manufacturing. *Economic & Political Weekly, 44*(10), 80–91.

Kathuria, S., and Bharadwaj, A. (1998). *Export quotas and policy constraints in the Indian textile and garment industries.* SASPR, World Bank, Working Paper, 2012.

Kraay, A. (1999). Exports and economic performance: Evidence from a panel of Chinese enterprises. *Revue d'Economie du Developpement, 1*(2), 183–207.

Ministry of Textiles. (2016–17). *Annual report.* New Delhi: Ministry of Textiles.

Roy, T. (1996). *Cloth and commerce: Textiles in colonial India.* New Delhi: Sage Publications.

Sastry, D. U. (1984, January–March). Capacity utilization in the cotton mill industry in India. *Indian Economic Review, 15*, 1–28.

United Nations Statistics Division. (2016). *UN Comtrade database.* New York: United Nations.

USITC. (2001). *Annual report.* Washington, DC: USITC.

Verma, S. (2002). *Export competitiveness of Indian textile and garment industry.* Indian Council for Research on International Economic Relations, Working Paper, 94.

Wagner, J. (2002). The causal effects of exports on firm size and labor productivity: First evidence from a matching approach. *Economics Letters, 77*(2), 287–292.

2 Conceptual outline

Introduction

In this chapter, the author makes an attempt to operationally define various factors affecting export competitiveness (EC). This may be achieved by understanding definitions, models, and theories specified by scientists, management thinkers, and researchers over a period of time. Literature is abundant with studies that identify the conceptual and theoretical mechanisms on select variables. It becomes also important to decide the methodology followed for literature review. Dhiman (2018); Dhiman and Sharma (2019); Mittal, Dhiman, and Lamba (2019); Dhiman, Chand, and Gupta (2018) highlight the process used to conduct the review and reveal that an important aspect before conducting the review is to finalize the method of selecting the research papers, time frame, and domain of research. In order to conduct the systematic review, the author has made use of a variety of scholarly journals and working papers in the field of manufacturing exports from reputed publishing houses such as Emerald, Elsevier, Inderscience, Sage, Taylor and Francis, Wiley-Blackwell, and others. The various platforms for getting access to papers are EBSCO and ProQuest. The literature has been accessed by using keywords such as 'export competitiveness,' 'Indian textile industry,' and 'comparative advantage.' The author uses the relevant literature published between 1991 and 2018.

The comparative advantage gained by a nation depends upon various factors such as labour and capital, which are important determinants included in the present book. The Heckscher-Ohlin (H-O) theory explained the reasons for comparative advantage differences among the various nations. According to H-O theory, different nations have different factor requirements in terms of labour and capital used in manufacturing products and services. This theory emphasized that a labour-intensive nation should focus on producing labour-intensive goods, and a nation with higher capital-intensity should focus on producing capital-intensive goods. Previous studies have also focused on identifying the specialization of a country. Since the U.S. is a capital-intensive country, it is likely to be an exporter of capital-intensive goods and an importer of those goods that require other factors such as labour, which is scarce. However, the empirical findings were opposite to this (Leontief, 1953). Other foreign trade theories in the literature have focused on the competitiveness of a nation, which is examined by the decrease in the real effective exchange rate (REER) (Boltho, 1996) and by minimizing unit labour cost (ULC) (Aiginger, 2009). Michael Porter, who leads the way for competitiveness theory, points out productivity as the best method of examining EC.

The above theories as well as literature have signified the importance of variables such as labour productivity (LP) and capital productivity (CP). Growth in LP and CP results in an increase in EC (Kordalska and Olczyk, 2014). So the competitiveness in terms of productivity parameters such as labour and capital needs to be examined. Hence, it becomes imperative to study LP and CP. Another reason for including LP and CP in the present book is that the textile industry is both labour and capital intensive, as large numbers of workers and updated technology are essential for the production of clothing. Since the clothing industry is labour intensive, ULC is also one of the crucial variables for the production of clothing. ULC is most frequently used for examining the cost competitiveness of a nation and, for this reason, is considered in the present book. Exchange rate (ER) and REER are other key determinants identified in the present book, and there is a need to identify the relationship among EC, ER, and REER, as this relationship has not been comprehensively examined at the industry level (Ito and Shimizu, 2015). Hence it also becomes imperative to study both ER and REER. Also, the literature suggests that raw material is one of the major strengths that textile industry carries, but raw material is out of the purview in the present book. This is because of the export-focused nature of the book. Including the aspects of raw material availability would have added a production-oriented dimension, deviating from the main aspect of the book, i.e. exports. Moreover, adding the data pertaining production of raw material for 24 years would have made the study more cumbersome.

In this chapter, an effort has been made to draw some conclusions on the basis of views expressed by previous researchers. The definitions provided by previous researchers on the select variables and interrelationships among them are also discussed in this chapter.

Export competitiveness

Previous studies have also made an attempt to examine the relationship between EC and productivity (Grossman and Helpman, 1991; Rivera-Batiz and Romer, 1991). EC is considered one of the most popular tools for the measurement of country competitiveness (Kordalska and Olczyk, 2014). There are several definitions of EC provided by previous researchers on the basis of levels and intent of analysis. EC is the ability of the nation to make and sell goods and services in overseas markets at prices and quality that certify long-term feasibility and sustainability (Farole, Reis, and Wagle, 2010).

EC is also defined as the ability of a firm to deliver products and services at the desired location and in the form desired by overseas buyers at competitive prices compared to other potential suppliers. Some researchers have defined competitiveness in relation to productivity, which in turn is a function of several factors such as cost. So competitiveness can also be defined in terms of LP, CP, and ULC. High rates of productivity growth are often regarded as a way of strengthening competitiveness (Durand and Giorno, 1987). Competitiveness can also be defined in relation to the sales, i.e. larger export share in the world market. It can be concluded that all the definitions of competitiveness admit productivity growth and capital formation as determinants of long-run competitiveness.

Countries engage freely in international trade because different nations are associated with different kinds of specializations (Krugman and Obstfeld, 2003). The theory of absolute advantage provided by Adam Smith in 1876 supports this fact and states that a nation can improve its wealth if it is specialized in manufacturing products and services that have an absolute cost advantage as compared to the other nations and should import those products and services that carry absolute cost disadvantage. This theory of absolute advantage had certain limitations also, because a country will not import any product or service in case it carries an absolute advantage in all goods and services it produces. This limitation was overcome by theory of comparative advantage advocated by Ricardo. The theory stated that a nation should specialize in the goods which can be produced more economically as compared to other nations (Krugman and Obstfeld, 2003). It means that despite absolute cost disadvantages in manufacturing the products and services, a nation can export products that carry the smallest absolute disadvantages and import goods carrying the largest absolute disadvantage. Hence competitiveness is an important factor for a country to survive in the international market.

The reasons for such comparative advantage gained by a nation also depend upon various factors such as labour and capital, which are important determinants included in the present book. Heckscher-Ohlin theory explained the reasons for comparative advantage differences between various nations. As per Heckscher-Ohlin theory, different nations require different factor requirements in terms of labour and capital which are used in manufacturing products and services.

Previous researchers have made an attempt to examine the competitiveness at various levels, such as (Jones, 1994; Murtha and Lenway, 1994) on the country level, (Uchikawa, 1999) on the regional level, (Roth and Morrison, 1992; Mitchell, Shaver, and Yeung, 1993) on the industry level, and (Pillania, 2006; Srivastava, 2006) on the firm level. In the existing body of knowledge, it is found that countries can never be competitive as a whole. Some industries can be more export competitive in comparison to the other ones. It becomes essential to consider the competitiveness of particular industries. Moreover, a number of factors such as labour and CP impact the EC, thus it is important for an industry to study and identify those factors and formulate appropriate strategies for improving competitiveness. So the competitiveness in terms of productivity parameters such as labour and capital also needs to be examined. Considering the importance of productivity in the literature, the present book examines various factor intensities in terms of labour and CP gained by India for the period of the study so that the competitiveness of India can be examined, and subsequently the recommendations are provided to the industry.

In the present volume, the EC has been examined by taking a share of textile exports in output. Three indicators of EC, i.e. share of India's textile exports in its total exports, the share of India's textile exports in world textile exports, and the ratio of India's textile exports to its output (export propensity of the Indian textile industry) has been calculated. However, in order to understand the influence of select variables on EC, the share of textile exports in its total output is taken, which is relatively a better indicator and reveals the competence of the nation to export textiles out of its domestic production.

Labour productivity

LP is a primary indicator of business performance and is also a significant indicator of the economic growth of a nation. In the existing body of knowledge, the importance of continuous productivity growth to survive in the competitive market is widely acknowledged (Joshi and Singh, 2010). Increase in LP completely translates into growth in EC. Therefore, studying LP becomes essential in theoretical and in applicative terms. Mark defined productivity as an output of the physical or factual volume of products and services associated with the physical or factual quantities of input (Mark, 1971, p.7). The inputs which are used during the production process primarily comprise two major parts, viz labour and capital. Study to examine the LP in the manufacturing industries is an area of interest to both economists and policy makers. Several authors have indicated the importance of the LP to ensure the competitiveness of the manufacturing industry in the world market (Ma, Liu, and Mills, 2016). High LP in the manufacturing industry facilitates sustainable growth and economic development of a nation. This, as a result, stimulates the export growth. A few authors have also focussed on the quality of the labour and its influence on technical progress. This, in turn, helps in achieving higher LP growth (Fox and Smeets, 2011). In addition to the quality of the labour, the synergetic effect in the labour can also help achieving higher productivity rates (Devaro, 2008).

There are several definitions of LP in the literature, but many of them are complex in nature. Due to complex definitions of the LP, different models and points of view have been developed at different levels. Measuring productivity by an index number approach is one view point and is widely used. This method of calculating productivity makes use of dividing an output quantity index by an input quantity index in order to get an index of productivity (Caves, Christensen, and Diewert, 1982a, 1982b). LP has been defined in several ways, such as the value of gross output per worker (Taymaz, 2002). One definition of LP in the literature is the output and input ratio, and it has been used as a measurement tool to examine LP (Ma et al., 2016). This approach has been applied by several other studies on the clothing industry in India (Bheda, Narag, and Singla, 2003; Joshi, Ishtiaque, and Jain, 2005). The empirical calculation of productivity was initially carried out by Stigler (1947). Stigler defined productivity as the ratio of output and the sum of labour input. LP is reflected as total product output and total input ratio at the industry level from an economic viewpoint. In the background of this description, LP indicates the quantity of output produced per unit of labour and time.

There are several measures to calculate the labour input. Some measures found in the literature are in terms of a total number of man-hours and the total number of employees. The biggest shortcoming for man-hours is the unavailability of such data, and moreover, the personnel departments may not be in the situation to have authentic data for a number of man-hours (Moon, 1982). Due to such shortcomings, several authors have used a total number of employees as labour input to calculate the LP (Subrahmanya, 2006). The gross value added (GVA) of the production per employee over a certain time period is also used to reflect the LP (Ma et al., 2016). The National Productivity Council (NPC) also uses GVA and a number of employees involved as the method of calculating the LP. The total number of employees in the manufacturing is considered as labour input. Shah, Syed, and Shaikh (2013) also define LP as value added per worker.

The production of a good requires different inputs in terms of labour, capital, energy, and materials. So it becomes essential to examine the productivity trends of such inputs. Productivity may be regarded differently by different people. To workers, productivity means to accelerate their work pattern. To union leaders, productivity is perceived as an occasion to negotiate for better wages. For consumers, productivity is better goods at lower costs. However, productivity in terms of labour can be defined as the ratio of output to one or more inputs utilized in the manufacturing process. In a country like India, in which majority of the industries are still labour intensive, it becomes very critical to study the trends in the LP, specifically in textile industry which is labour intensive. LP can also be defined as the output-to-input ratio. The input in terms of labour is calculated by using the data related to the number of employees engaged (Subrahmanya, 2006).

The most important factor impacting the competitiveness of an industry is productivity trends and growth. One such significant variable of productivity can be LP. Growth in LP results in an increase in EC (Kordalska and Olczyk, 2014). Therefore, rising productivity indicates rising competence of a variety of resources of manufacturing or improved results with smaller efforts. However, in the existing body of knowledge, it is found that India is far behind in terms of LP as compared to nations such as China, Taiwan, South Korea, etc. For illustration, in case of gents' shirts, the LP for India is smallest at 9.1 pieces per machine per day, as compared to China's productivity level of 14.0 (Rangarajan, 2005). So for a labour-intensive industry, it becomes important to achieve higher productivity levels to compete in the world market. The improvement in productivity not only adds to the competitiveness but also encourages the growth in an economy. The explanations, as discussed above, present the conceptual foundations for the relationship between exports and productivity.

Capital productivity

There was a time when LP was considered one of the major drivers of productivity, especially in the labour-intensive industries. But with the passage of time and subsequent liberalization of trade, technology transfer has brought the way for considering the CP as another determinant of improving the competitiveness in the world market. This is because of certain textile products that are capital intensive, such as man-made fibres. Many of the developed nations have achieved higher levels of CP. So investment in capital becomes important for an organization to stay competitive in the international market. However, the result of Hashim (2005) points out that there are only 17 percent world-class manufacturing plants in India. The state of affairs in the domestic sector was worse, as only 9 percent of plants are advanced by the Indian standard, and none of the plants are as per the global standards. This has seriously affected the productivity of capital. Improvement in capital minimizes the usage of manual labour as CP also improves the productivity trends in labour. So the CP has a vital role to play in examining the productivity of a nation. As already highlighted, earlier researchers had to deal with labour productivities, but nowadays, productivity analysis is often supplemented by examining the trends in the CP as well. The CP explains how well the resources of a business are being used to produce input. After examining the trends in productivity, these can be used for planning, monitoring, and getting better performance from a firm.

While examining the relationship between exports and productivity, the hypothesis can be that the firms with higher productivity are more likely to perform better in the competitive world markets. This is in line with the conclusion drawn from international trade theory, which says that the firms self-select into the export markets (Bernard and Jensen, 1999). In addition, this kind of justification is also in line with the traditional Heckscher-Ohlin notions, which suggest that improved factor endowments and production technologies impact the trends of trade of specific products (Pugel, 2004). In line with the Heckscher-Ohlin argument, exporting firms in European parts of the country such as Germany were found to be exporting more capital-intensive goods. This indicates the positive impact of CP on the export performance (Bernard and Wagner, 1997). A study conducted on Indian exporting firms also indicates the importance of CP on export performance (Pant, 1993). In the present book, it is hypothesized that CP would have a positive impact on the export performance of the textile and clothing industry. The explanations as discussed present the conceptual foundations for the relationship between exports and productivity.

CP can be measured as output divided by the capital input (Thor, 1986). CP examines the output produced per unit of capital. Gross fixed capital formation can be used as the measure of examining the capital input. CP can be measured as the ratio of GVA to gross fixed capital. The increase in CP indicates that with the passage of time, more output can be produced with a decrease in the amounts of inputs required or with the same inputs or same output with lesser inputs. The industry's production process is regarded as highly efficient if an industry has high productivity. This is because the industry can generate more output with the same level of input as compared to the competitors. NPC, Government of India, examines CP by dividing GVA at constant prices by the estimated fixed capital. It has been found that CP is a significant factor to promote export growth. As per the report of NPC, the CP of the textile and clothing industry improved from Rs. 0.38 per unit of every rupee invested for the duration of 1995–96 to Rs. 0.78 by year 2005–06.

The enhancement of CP does not mean that very few workers are required in a firm. The increase in CP at the firm or industry level indicates that with the introduction of new technology, fewer workers are needed to meet production goals (Singh, 2010). Capitalistic nations always focus on the so-called efficiency factors of production. Such factors of production are used as inputs to the process of production. In the conventional neo-classical growth model, both labour and capital are regarded as the main dependencies. The competitiveness of a firm can be enhanced by improving the efficiency of the key factor input such as capital. The return on invested capital is very important for a firm to be regarded as successful in the economic sense. CP can be defined as the ratio of output to capital input and indicates value added per unit of capital (Subrahmanya, 2006).

A number of previous studies have made an attempt to examine the productivity trends of the manufacturing industry of India (Balakrishnan and Pushpangadan, 1994; Srivastava, 2006; Goldar, 2004). A few of these researchers also studied the influence of the reforms of 1991 on the expansion of productivity of industries. Some researchers established that economic reform created a positive influence on the growth of productivity in the manufacturing industries (Majumdar, 1996; Pattnayak and Thangavelu, 2005). However, a few studies found that economic reforms have negatively influenced productivity growth in India (Balakrishnan, Pushpangadan, and Babu, 2000; Goldar and Kumar, 2003). A number of productivity measures have been proposed over the years, depending on the inputs and outputs used. Among them, CP is another widely used measure. The previous study examined the CP of the Indian textile industry highlights that CP in the

'Textiles' group grew at a swift pace. However, in the 'Textile Products' group CP was negative during the post–World Trade Organisation period (Narula and Nanda, 2011). This fall in the CP is a serious concern because the world market is becoming more and more competitive, and in order to survive in this highly competitive market, the CP needs to be improved. The improvement of CP in the Indian textile industry will enable to tap the growing domestic market and also to increase its share in the world market. So it becomes important to study CP of an industry. Hence CP is selected as another determinant in the present book.

Unit labour cost

The clothing industry is labour intensive, as large number of workers are essential for the production of clothing. Therefore, ULC is one of the crucial variables for the production of clothing. ULC is the most frequently used for examining the cost competitiveness of a nation. In the highly competitive world market, the exports of labour-intensive products will lose its market-place in comparison to the other nations possessing the competitive advantage of labour cost (Thornhill, 1988). Therefore, it is important for India to possess a labour cost competitiveness advantage, especially in labour-intensive industries like textiles. Labour cost is a significant constituent of the overall manufacturing cost, which can make up for the unpleasant influence of any other macroeconomic imbalances including ER, other foreign trade policies, etc. It is assumed that the exporting firms depend more on labour cost-cutting methods in order to achieve competitiveness. Therefore, the firms that decide to export would rely on labour cost as a vital factor for decision making. Firms that have low labour cost are more likely to become exporters as compared to firms that are unable to manufacture at low labour cost. The Heckscher-Ohlin model becomes the basis for this argument of comparative advantage gained due to low factor cost. A nation can gain a comparative advantage if it produces the goods more cheaply compared to the other suppliers in the market.

Theoretically, the competitiveness of exports increases with a decrease in ULC and vice versa. A country having higher labour cost is expected to have less attractiveness as a supplier of textile and clothing products. Therefore, ULC should have a negative influence on textile and clothing exports (Tsang and Au, 2008). As highlighted by Kannapiran and Fleming (1999), a nation has a comparative advantage over the others if that nation can do so at a lower cost. The approach of considering the costs involved is used in the estimation of competitiveness, assuming that the changes in the price level are determined largely by the intensity of the manufacturing costs involved, mainly labour costs. So ULCs are also considered in examining the competitiveness in this volume. Authors in the previous studies have also mentioned labour cost as a significant determinant of international competitiveness. A study by Abraham and Sasikumar (2011) confirms that international competitiveness of the industries in developing economies is still dependent on the comparative advantage gained in terms of labour cost. One of the reasons for such dependency can be attributed to the fact of lack of technological developments of these nations. A number of previous studies have also confirmed the lack of technological development of Indian textile firms (Bedi and Cororaton, 2008; USITC, 2001). However, such a strategy of dependency on cheap labour cost is unlikely to sustain the competitive markets for the longer run.

ULC is measured as a ratio of employment cost to value added of the manufacturing industries using data obtained from the Annual Survey of Industries (ASI). Abraham and Sasikumar (2011) examined labour cost by using salaries, wages, and other labour charges. Theoretically, increase in ULCs results in the reduction of exports by increasing the relative prices of domestic countries. The advantage of taking ULCs as a determinant of EC is that ULC enables the researcher to calculate the influence of variations in the production cost on EC (Ito and Shimizu, 2015).

It is a well-known fact that with the increase in the scale of manufacturing, the mean costs are likely to decrease. Hence the EC of the firm increases. As India is known for its comparatively abundant factor, namely labour, India must gain a comparative advantage. Moreover, comparative advantage cannot be gained only through economical labour in terms of low wage rate per worker. The countries which have higher labour costs will be ranked last in terms of their priority for being a supplier of textile and clothing products. Several nations have achieved competitiveness by minimizing the labour costs. The developing nations acquire cheap and skilful labour. This is one of the competitive advantages of developing nations over developed ones in clothing production (Tsang and Au, 2008). Hence, the developing nations would have a comparative advantage in the clothing export to the other countries. So, India, being a developing country, should exploit these favourable conditions.

A study conducted by NPC (2010), New Delhi, highlights that India is far ahead in terms of labour cost per hour as compared to other developed countries. The analysis reveals that India's labour cost per hour in 2004 is US$0.6 in comparison to the other developed nations such as the U.S., with US$15.1 and industrialized economies such as Taiwan with US$7.1, South Korea with US$5.7, Hong Kong having US$5.1, and China with US$0.9. However, contradictory studies are also found in the literature. The previous studies indicate that India has a comparative advantage in terms of labour cost as compared to the developed countries, but labour cost in other competing countries is much lower in comparison to India. So it can be concluded that low labour cost is not sufficient to achieve competitive advantage in the clothing industry. This cost disadvantage is due to major factors such as higher labour cost and declining trends in labour and CP in comparison to the competitors. While India and China do not gain labour cost competitiveness, the share of China in the global garments trade has improved in 2008 to more than 33 percent. However, India, despite having lesser wage rate in comparison to China, is not able to achieve the two-digit mark, which is a serious problem. Vietnam also achieved competitiveness in the textile and garments trade due to the lower labour costs. As a result, Vietnam is now the fifth largest U.S. supplier of clothing products (Tsang and Au, 2008). Bangladesh also achieved higher growth rates in their clothing exports. The major determinant for this higher growth is low labour costs (Bhattacharya and Rahman, 2000). Vietnam, Cambodia, and Pakistan are other garment exporters in addition to Bangladesh taking benefit of small labour costs at 33, 37, and 38 cents per hour, respectively (Kathuria, 2013).

Total labour costs are examined by taking the total compensation to employees, which includes wages and salaries, as well as other benefits in cash. A study conducted by Tsang and Au (2007) also examined the labour cost from dividing the wages and salaries by the number of employees during the select years. ULC represents the average wage per worker who works in the textile and clothing industry. The Indian labour costs are among the lowest as compared with the other parts of the world. However, these are balanced by higher prices for other inputs, and as a result, LP also declines. However, it must be noted that only cheap labour in terms of small wage per employee does not lead in gaining the comparative cost advantage, but low wages in terms of the LP is more important. A study conducted by the McKinsey Global Institute (MGI) (2004) indicated that the productivity of Indian exporters' was only 35 percent as compared to U.S. levels. However, the other neighbouring country such as China had 55 percent. A study conducted by Ito and Shimizu (2015) also confirms the importance of the productivity. The study highlighted that India's labour costs are 30 percent lower as compared to China, but its productivity is less than half of China's in some product categories (MGI, 2001). The importance of productivity in relation to labour costs is identified by other authors also. Stengg (2001) confirms that in the clothing industry, the per-hour cost of labour in Indonesia, India, and China ranges US$0.24 to 0.62. However, in the European Union, the hourly labour costs ranges from US$4.5 in Portugal to US$23 in Denmark. These European nations may possess this competitive disadvantage in labour costs, but these are, to a degree, offset by higher levels of labour productivity, which is expressed as value added per employee.

It can be noted that the impact of appreciation and depreciation of ER can also be reduced if labour costs are lower in comparison to the other countries. Empirical evidence in this regard was provided by Stengg (2001). This study confirms that the considerable appreciation of the ER will not drastically decrease Chinese competitiveness because of the low cost and increase in labour. So labour costs are always the centre of attraction in any labour intensive industry, provided they are productive as well. This has an impact on creating demand for the product in the world markets. So it becomes very important to examine the ULCs. So considering the importance of ULC in the existing body of knowledge, it becomes very important to include ULC as a determinant of EC. The explanations given present the conceptual foundations for the relationship between exports competitiveness and ULC.

Exchange rate

In addition to labour and CP, ER is another important determinant of competitiveness of the industry. The policy makers, over a period time, have long been worried with the impact of variations in the ER on the growth of the economy and competitiveness. The survey of published literature in the field of variations of ER gives some interesting viewpoints. The Mundell-Fleming model highlights that appreciation in the ER would damage exports and support imports for small open economies. This theory and its recommendations suppose that markets are perfect and the prices of commodities are set by the global markets. Athukorala (1991) argues that, in changing levels, exporters sustain competitiveness in global markets by reducing their profit margins in the face of an appreciating currency. A study by Banik (2008) also indicates that the EC is primarily a function of variables such as the ER. The Indian textile and clothing industry is an export-oriented industry, so the fluctuations in ER are very important.

The ER can be defined as the rate at which one currency can be exchanged for another currency. This is extracted from various issues of *International Financial Statistics* of the IMF and *Handbook of Statistics on Indian Economy* (RBI, 1991–2017). The ER is also defined as a number of units of domestic currency per unit of the foreign currency (Taymaz, 2002) and in terms of home currency worth per unit of overseas currency, which is used in the present book for the analysis. The reforms in the ER played a vital part to promote the Indian exports. It was way back in July 1991 that India devalued its currency by almost 19 percent. Such reforms in the ER resulted in positive export growth. The exports grew from –1.1 percent in 1991–92 to 20.2 percent in 1993–94. They further increased to 20.7 percent in 1995–96 as a result of reforms.

The changes in the ER of countries across the world have influenced the prices of their exports in global markets and, as a result, impact the EC (Sharma and Dhiman, 2014, 2016; Ito and Shimizu, 2015). Theoretically, the ER depreciation would encourage exports and limit imports, while appreciation of the ER will be unfavourable to exports and would support imports. Evidence in previous studies reveals that depreciation in the ER has a positive effect on exports; this is what the macro-economic theories suggest. The depreciation in the rupee will make the exports cheaper, and hence this will increase the demand for exported goods in the world market. Jaussaud and Rey (2012) investigated the impact of ER on the exports of Japan to China and the U.S. The period of analysis ranged from 1971 to 2007. The findings of analysis using the vector error correction model (VECM) highlighted that appreciation of the yen and rise in ER volatility decreased the exports of Japan. Similar findings were also reported by Biselli (2009). The study indicates that the nominal ER is extremely important in all international trading transactions. The nations with undervalued currencies facilitate the overseas buyers to use their relatively overvalued currency to buy 'cheap' in the domestic market. The Cotton Textile Export Promotion Council (TEXPROCIL) also brings out an important fact that unfavourable ER of Indian rupee in comparison to Sri Lanka, Indonesia, and Pakistan, where the inequality was about 5 percent to 6 percent in the earlier periods, is now more than 20 percent. This has an unfavourable effect on Indian exports.

However, there is a lack of agreement on the subject of the influence of appreciation or depreciation in the ER on economic determinants like exports. A few studies in this regard are found in literature which indicate that ER does not have the biggest influence on Indian exports (Sarkar, 1992; Srinivasan, 1998). Some studies established a significant relationship between export performance and ER (Sarkar, 1997). The Indian currency fluctuated against the U.S. dollar in the year 2008. This negatively impacted the Indian trade performance. In the year 2007–08, the appreciation in the Indian rupee against the U.S. dollar resulted in lesser export growth for the Indian textiles and clothing industry. Similar findings were also reported by Taymaz in 2002. It is also observed that ER only does not influence the export growth, but the demand for the quality product is another vital factor. During the post-reform regime, the exports were not only led by the appreciation or depreciation in the ER, but the demand of the commodity also played a key role in explaining export performance at a disaggregate level during 1960–1999.

Another situation is also found in the literature in which the exports increased during the time of currency appreciation. The literature suggests that this can be because of many reasons. One possible reason can be increasing external demand for a commodity. Increase in the productivity could be another reason for such rise. Pricing-to-market policies could have countered the negative impact of appreciation in the currency (Abeysinghe and Yeok, 1998).

In the existing body of knowledge, there are studies on exploring the influence of ER on exports. A few studies present positive while some negative effects of the depreciation of the home currency, while some studies provide no effect of a rise in ER on the exports. So the mixed impact of the ER can be seen in the literature. One possible reason for this negative influence might be that whenever there is a depreciation of the rupee against the key destination countries, the confidence in the economy also decreases. This, as a result, may lead the investors to pull out their investment, in turn decreasing the exports of Japan to China and the U.S. and exports from India. However, Lee (1999) discovers no significant impact. In spite of the inconsistent results in the literature, the firms strongly believe that the changes in the ERs have real effects. In fact, firms over and over again spend time and resources to hedge against risk associated with the ER. These mixed results are also supported by Shah (2013). The study concludes that at an international level, there is lack of consensus on whether ERs have an impact on real economic variables like exports.

From the discussion, it is found that since the ER is among the major determinants of exports, so the change in ER impacts the export sector. Therefore, the present book is an attempt to relate the exports of Japan to China and the U.S. of textiles and clothing amongst other determinants with the changes in the ER. The results of the previous studies, as indicated, regarding the competitiveness of India's manufactured exports found India in a noticeably poor group in terms of export performance during the 1960s. However, with the changes in the ER against U.S. dollars during the 1970s, India experienced progressive improvement in international competitiveness due to such changes in the ER. The explanations discussed present the conceptual foundations for the relationship between exports competitiveness and ER. It would be interesting to study the part of ER fluctuations in examining the competitiveness of Indian exports. It would be worth testing through empirical investigation whether and to what degree the variations in the ER affect the EC of India.

Real effective exchange rate

The REER can be defined as the weighted mean value of a currency in comparison to the currencies of the key trading partners of a nation, adjusted with inflation. REER reveals the relative movement of prices at home and abroad and has a major influence on export performance. REER examines the competitiveness of the home currency against the foreign currency. REER reveals the health of the economy of a nation. The critical determinant for examining the EC is changing prices. The REER is considered the most commonly used tool for examining competitiveness (Kordalska and Olczyk, 2014). The various industry reports time and again talk about EC in the light of ER variations, along with other determinants, and for that reason recommend that REER may be appropriate in the Indian context. In particular, the Reserve Bank of India (RBI) also recommended that variations in the value of the rupee impacted the Indian industries disproportionately. REER includes the weighted real exchange rate between a nation and its major trading partners. A key aspect decisive in examining the performance of exports lies in the changes of its REER. It is measured as the nominal effective exchange rate multiplied by the key trading partner price index and divided by the price index of India. Upadhyay and Roy (2016) define REER as a weighted average of a nation's currency in comparison to a basket of other key currencies. The weights are examined by evaluating the comparative trade balances. RBI publishes REER data monthly. From that, a quarterly average of REER value is estimated, and afterwards, the percentage change is examined.

Many of the previous studies have used REER as an indicator of competitiveness on the basis of their calculations on fixed or periodically updated weighting patterns. It is well known that the appreciation of the REER minimized the demand for exports. The results of Chan, Au, and Sarkar (2008) also indicate that the REER plays a vital part in deciding the quantity of textile exports. In case of appreciation and depreciation of the Indian rupee against an overseas currency, there will be a rise or fall in the exports. Theoretically, a stronger REER indicates that the home nation is less competitive, and weak REER indicates that the home nation is more competitive. So appreciation of REER indicates a loss in competitiveness, and depreciation indicates an increase in competitiveness. Upadhyay and Roy (2016) support this theory. The results of the study indicates that the export growth in rupee terms reduced to 14.60 percent in 2007–2008 as a result of appreciation in REER that appreciated by 7.44 percent. Kordalska and Olczyk (2014) study the impact of REER variations on the export of China from 1978–2005 using the VECM. The outcome of empirical analysis suggests that REER negatively impacts exports. Cheung and Sengupta (2013) investigated the effect of REER on the export of Indian companies in the non-financial sector. The study period was from 2000–2010. The findings of the study using multiple regression confirm a strong negative influence of the appreciation of the ER and ER volatility on exports. The authors studied the impact of REER of the Indian rupee on the export of the non-financial sector of Indian companies. The time period selected was from 2000–2010. The results of the multiple regression indicate a strong negative influence of the appreciation of the REER on the exports.

Consensus on the impact of REER on the EC is missing in the literature. Some of the contradictory studies are discussed in this section of the chapter. Previous studies examining the impact of REER on EC in different nations are carried out by Sweidan (2013) and Hooy, Law, and Chan (2015). However, there is no agreement in the previous studies concerning the findings of the study. Previous studies carried out by Caglayan and Demir (2013) indicated the positive influence of REER on the exports. However, other studies found the negative impact of REER on exports (Kemal and Qadir, 2005; Cheung and Sengupta, 2013). Some of the previous studies concluded that there was no impact of REER on exports in the long duration (Fang and Miller, 2007; Nyeadi, Atiga, and Atogenzoya, 2014).

REER is one of the variables that has an effect on the export growth of a nation. This fact is also reported by previous studies, and the findings of their study are discussed in this section. Srinivasan (1998) investigated overall patterns of export performance of India since 1951. The author also examined the EC since the mid-1980s. The study highlighted REER as an important determinant in explaining the performance of exports. Depreciation of REER makes the exported commodity cheaper in terms of foreign currency in the world market. This, as a result, increases the demand for such products in the global market. This encourages the exporters, and therefore the exporters would be willing to deliver more commodities with the depreciation of the nation's currency. Hence, a negative relationship between REER and volume of export is expected. This result is also supported by a study conducted by Veeramani (2008), which reports a negative association between REER and total merchandise exports of India. A few other studies on REER and their influence on exports also indicate the strong impact of REER on exports. The econometric findings of the study indicate that REER depreciation had a significant influence on the select products. The results further confirm that the selected commodity exports are highly elastic with respect to REER.

Another study by Veeramani (2008) examines the impact of REER policies on Cameroon's agricultural EC. The study points out that a 10 percent depreciation of REER encourages about 1 percent increase of cocoa export. As cited by Srinivasan (1998, p. 211), there is a strong relationship between the depreciation of REER and growth in export during the 1970s and the late 1980s. A few studies conducted in Ghana and India by Fosu (1992) and Sharma (2001) also highlight that REER has a significant negative relationship with the growth of exports. Similar findings were also reported by Kaur (2007). The study indicates that REER, along with time, positively and non-significantly influenced the EC and explained about 89.7 percent variations. Bhatt (2008) investigated trade competitiveness of India with respect to its competitors and also studies the efficacy of the REER strategy on the competitiveness of the trade. The study highlights that when REER appreciated, export price competitiveness improved, but the competitiveness in terms of profitability declined.

From the discussion, it can be concluded that the literature is abundant with the studies that identify the conceptual and theoretical mechanisms on select variables. The theoretical background is based on Heckscher-Ohlin (H-O) theory that suggests that the competitiveness gained by a nation depends upon various factors such as labour and capital, which are important determinants included in the present book. H-O theory explained the reasons for comparative advantage differences between various nations. As per H-O theory, different nations require different factor requirements in terms of labour and capital used in manufacturing products and services.

The discussion reveals that the most important determinant of competitiveness is productivity. The industry must put in large efforts to increase the productivity levels in order to increase the EC. Higher productivity trends and lower labour costs will definitely determine which countries will win or lose in the global market. However, previous productivity studies also indicated that the productivity of Indian textile firms has decreased due to lack of advanced technology, less investment per machine, fewer machines per firm, and poor infrastructure (Joshi et al., 2005; Rangarajan, 2005).

In addition to this, interrelationship among labour cost, ER, and REER are also found with the EC. The previous studies by Bernard and Jensen (1997, 1999) on the United States and by Aw, Chung, and Roberts (1998) on

Taiwan and Korea have all examined the exports-productivity linkage and finds that productivity trends in an industry impacts the EC. The rise in ULC and appreciation of the domestic currency decrease exports by increasing the relative prices of the domestic country. The exchange-rate depreciation encourages exports, but the ER risk plays an important role in impacting export-price competitiveness. This results in the sluggish growth of exports. It is evident that there are number of studies that investigate the relationship between exports and productivity. The previous studies have also made an attempt to examine the relationship between EC and its determinants, such as labour and CP, that impact the EC, thus it is important for an industry to critically examine these factors and formulate appropriate strategies for improving competitiveness.

Concluding remarks

The arguments provided by previous studies and theories can be beneficial in the formulation of hypotheses. As per Heckscher-Ohlin theory, the requirements of nations differ in terms of labour and capital used in manufacturing products and services. This theory emphasized that a labour-intensive nation should focus on producing labour-intensive goods and a nation with higher capital intensity should focus on producing capital-intensive goods. Since the textile industry is both labour and capital intensive, it therefore becomes pertinent to understand whether the Indian textile industry and its two groups are productive in terms of labour and capital. Moreover, the impact of labour and capital productivity over EC needs to be determined. Literature also reveals that ULC is most frequently used for examining the cost competitiveness of a nation and may impact the competitiveness of exports. Similarly, ER and REER are other key variables identified, and a previous study by Ito and Shimizu, 2015 also emphasizes the need to identify the relationship between EC, ER and REER. Thus, it is quite evident that all the select determinants have an impact over EC for the textile industry and its two groups. Taking in to consideration these facts, it can be assumed that there is long-run relationship among the select variables for the Indian textile industry and its two groups.

References

Abeysinghe, T., and Yeok, L. T. (1998). Exchange rate appreciation and export competitiveness: The case of Singapore. *Applied Economics*, 30(1), 51–55.

Abraham, V., and Sasikumar, S. K. (2011). Labor cost and export behavior of firms in Indian textile and clothing industry. *Economics, Management and Financial Markets*, 6(1), 258–282.

Aiginger, K. (2009). Speed of change and growth of manufacturing. In *Structural change and economic growth: Reconsidering the Austrian 'old-structures/high-performance' paradox*. Vienna: Austrian Institute of Economic Research (WIFO).

Athukorala, P. (1991). Exchange rate pass-through: The case of Korean exports of manufactures. *Economic Letters, 35,* 79–84.

Aw, B., Chung, S., and Roberts, M. (1998). *Productivity and the decision to export market: Micro evidence from Taiwan and South Korea.* National Bureau of Economic Research, Working Paper, *6558.*

Balakrishnan, P., and Pushpangadan, K. (1994). Total factor productivity in manufacturing industry: A fresh look. *Economic & Political Weekly, 29,* 2028–2035.

Balakrishnan, P., Pushpangadan, K., and Babu, S. M. (2000). Trade liberalization and productivity growth in manufacturing: Evidence from firm level panel data. *Economic & Political Weekly, 35*(41), 3679–3682.

Banik, N. (2008). India's exports: An analysis. *ASCI Journal of Management, 37*(2), 151–163.

Bedi, S. J., and Cororaton, C. B. (2008). *Cotton-textile-apparel sectors of India situations and challenges faced markets.* The International Food Policy Research Institute, Discussion Paper, 801.

Bernard, A. B., and Jensen, J. B. (1999). Exceptional exporter performance: Cause, effect, or both. *Journal of International Economics, 47*(1), 1–25.

Bernard, A. B., and Wagner, J. (1997). Exports and success in German manufacturing. *Review of World Economics, 133*(1), 134–157.

Bhatt, P. R. (2008). India's trade competitiveness and exchange rate policy. *The Journal of Applied Economic Research, 2*(3), 247–268.

Bhattacharya, D., and Rahman, M. (2000). *Experience with implementation of WTO-ATC and implications for Bangladesh.* Centre for Policy, Dialogue, 7.

Bheda, R., Narag, A. S., and Singla, M. L. (2003). Apparel manufacturing: A strategy for productivity improvement. *Journal of Fashion and Marketing Management, 7*(1), 12–22.

Biselli, M. (2009). *China's role in the global textile industry.* China Europe International Business School, Student Research Projects/Outputs, 39.

Boltho, A. (1996). The assessment: International competitiveness. *Oxford Review of Economic Policy, 12*(3), 1–16.

Caglayan, M., and Demir, F. (2013). Firm productivity, exchange rate movements, sources of finance, and export orientation. *World Development, 54,* 204–219.

Caves, D., Christensen, L., and Diewert, E. (1982a). The economic theory of index numbers and the measurement of input, output and productivity. *Econometrica, 50*(6), 1393–1414.

Caves, D., Christensen, L., and Diewert, E. (1982b). Multilateral comparisons of output, input and productivity using superlative index numbers. *The Economic Journal, 92*(365), 73–86.

Chan, E. M. H., Au, K. F., and Sarkar, M. K. (2008). Antecedents to India's textile exports: 1985–2005. *International Journal of Indian Culture and Business Management, 1*(3), 265–276.

Cheung, Y. W., and Sengupta, S. (2013). Impact of exchange rate movements on exports: An analysis of Indian non-financial sector firms. *Journal of International Money and Finance, 39,* 231–245.

Devaro, J. (2008). The effects of self-managed and closely managed teams on labor productivity and product quality: An empirical analysis of a cross-section of establishments. *Industrial Relations: A Journal of Economy and Society, 47*(4), 659–697.

Dhiman, R. (2018). Identifying the key indicators of financial stability and financial development: A review of financial service sector. *Asian Journal of Management Science and Applications*, *3*(4), 302–320.

Dhiman, R., Chand, P., and Gupta, S. (2018). Behavioural aspects influencing decision to purchase apparels amongst young Indian consumers. *FIIB Business Review*, *7*(3), 188–200.

Dhiman, R., and Sharma, M. (2019). Relation between labour productivity and export competitiveness of Indian textile industry: Cointegration and causality approach. *Vision: The Journal of Business Perspective*, *23*(1), 22–30.

Durand, M., and Giorno, C. (1987). Indicators of international competitiveness: Conceptual aspects and evaluation. *OECD Economic Studies*, *9*, 147–182.

Fang, W. S., and Miller, S. M. (2007). Exchange rate depreciation and exports: The case of Singapore revisited. *Applied Economics*, *39*(3), 273–277.

Farole, T., Reis, J. G., and Wagle, S. (2010). *Analyzing trade competitiveness–a diagnostics approach*. Washington, DC: The World Bank.

Fosu, K. Y. (1992). *The real exchange rate and Ghana's agricultural exports*. African Economic Research Consortium Research Paper, 9.

Fox, J., and Smeets, V. (2011). Does input quality drive measured differences in firm productivity? *International Economic Review*, *52*(4), 961–989.

Goldar, B. (2004). Indian manufacturing: Productivity trends in pre and post-reform periods. *Economic & Political Weekly*, *39*(46–47), 5033–5043.

Goldar, B., and Kumar, A. (2003). Import liberalisation and productivity growth in Indian manufacturing industries in the 1990s. *The Developing Economies*, *41*(4), 436–460.

Grossman, G., and Helpman, E. (1991). *Innovation and growth in the global economy*. Cambridge: MIT Press.

Hashim, D. A. (2005). Post-MFA: Making the textile and garment industry competitive. *Economic & Political Weekly*, *40*(2), 117–127.

Hooy, C. W., Law, S. H., and Chan, T. H. (2015). The impact of the Renminbi real exchange rate on ASEAN disaggregated exports to China. *Economic Modelling*, *47*, 253–259.

Ito, K., and Shimizu, J. (2015). Industry-level competitiveness, productivity and effective exchange rates in East Asia. *Asian Economic Journal*, *29*(2), 181–214.

Jaussaud, J., and Rey, S. (2012). Long-run determinants Japanese export to China and the United States: A sectoral analysis. *Pacific Economic Review*, *17*(1), 1–28.

Jones, G. (1994). Big business, management and competitiveness in twentieth century Britain. *Japan Business History Review*, *29*.

Joshi, P., Ishtiaque, S. M., and Jain, S. K. (2005). Competitiveness of Indian clothing in WTO era. *Asian Textile Journal*, *14*(12), 66–77.

Joshi, R. N., and Singh, S. P. (2010). Estimation of total factor productivity in the Indian garment industry. *Journal of Fashion Marketing and Management*, *14*(1), 145–160.

Kannapiran, C. A., and Fleming, M. (1999). *Competitiveness and comparative advantage of tree crop small-holdings in PNG*. University of New England, Australia, Working Paper, 99–10.

Kathuria, M. L. (2013). Analyzing competitiveness of clothing export sector of India and Bangladesh: Dynamic revealed comparative advantage approach. *Competitiveness Review: An International Business Journal*, *23*(2), 131–157.

Kaur, P. (2007). Growth acceleration in India. *Economic & Political Weekly*, 42(15), 1380–1386.

Kemal, M. A., and Qadir, U. (2005). Real exchange rate, exports, and imports movements: A trivariate analysis. *The Pakistan Development Review*, 44(2), 177–195.

Kordalska, A., and Olczyk, M. (2014). Impact of the manufacturing sector on the export competitiveness of European countries–a spatial panel analysis. *Comparative Economic Research*, 17(4), 105–121.

Krugman, P. R., and Obstfeld, M. (2003). *International economics: Theory and policy*. New York: HarperCollins.

Lee, J. (1999). The effect of exchange rate volatility on trade in durables. *Review of International Economics*, 7(2), 189–201.

Leontief, W. (1953). Domestic production and foreign trade: The American capital position re-examined. *Proceedings of the American Philosophical Society*, 97(4), 332–349.

Ma, L., Liu, C., and Mills, A. (2016). Construction labor productivity convergence: A conditional frontier approach. *Engineering, Construction and Architectural Management*, 23(3), 283–301.

Majumdar, S. K. (1996). Fall and rise of productivity in Indian industries: Has economic liberalisation had an impact? *Economic & Political Weekly*, 31(48), 46–53.

Mark, J. A. (1971). *Concept and measures of productivity in the meaning and measurement of productivity*. Bulletin of the Bureau of Labor Statistics, 1714.

MGI. (2001). *India: The growth imperative*. Washington, DC: McKinsey Global Institute.

MGI. (2004). *Apparel and textile trade report*. Washington, DC: McKinsey Global Institute.

Mitchell, W., Shaver, J. M., and Yeung, B. (1993). Performance following changes in international presence in domestic and transition industries. *Journal of International Business Studies*, 24(4), 647–670.

Mittal, A., Dhiman, R., and Lamba, P. (2019). Skill mapping for blue-collar employees and organisational performance: A qualitative assessment. *Benchmarking: An International Journal*, 26(4), 1255–1274.

Moon, Y. S. (1982). *Labor productivity: A search and confirmation of non-traditional determinants* (Doctoral dissertation). University of Oklahoma, Norman, OK.

Murtha, T. P., and Lenway, S. A. (1994). Country capability and the strategic state: How national political institutions affect multinational corporations' strategies. *Strategic Management Journal*, 15(S2), 113–129.

Narula, R., and Nanda, P. (2011). *Impact of WTO regime on Indian textile industry* (Doctoral dissertation). Guru Nanak Dev University, Amritsar.

NPC. (2010). *Annual report 2009–10*. New Delhi: National Productivity Council.

Nyeadi, J. D., Atiga, O., and Atogenzoya, C. A. (2014). The impact of exchange rate movement on export: Empirical evidence from Ghana. *International Journal of Academic Research in Accounting, Finance and Management Sciences*, 4(3), 41–48.

Pant, M. (1993). Export performance, transnational corporations and the manufacturing sector: A case study of India. *Indian Economic Review*, 28(1), 41–54.

Pattnayak, S. S., and Thangavelu, S. M. (2005). Economic reform and productivity growth in Indian manufacturing industries: An interaction of technical change and scale economics. *Economic Modelling*, 22(4), 601–615.

Pillania, R. K. (2006). Leveraging knowledge for sustainable competitiveness in SMEs. *International Journal of Globalisation and Small Business, 1*(4), 23–35.

Pugel, T. (2004). *International economics.* New York: McGraw Hill.

Rangarajan, K. (2005). International trade in textile and clothing post-MFA challenges & strategic consideration for India. *Foreign Trade Review, 39*(4), 3–23.

RBI. (1991–2017). *Handbook of statistics on Indian economy.* Reserve Bank of India. Retrieved from https://dbie.rbi.org.in/DBIE/dbie.rbi?site = home

Rivera-Batiz, L. A., and Romer, P. (1991). Economic integration and endogenous growth. *The Quarterly Journal of Economics, 106*(2), 531–555.

Roth, K., and Morrison, A. J. (1992). Implementing global strategy: Characteristics of global subsidiary mandates. *Journal of International Business Studies, 23*(4), 715–735.

Sarkar, P. (1992). An econometric study of trade flows: A case study of ESCAP countries. *Indian Economic Journal, 32*(3), 15–23.

Sarkar, P. (1997). Foreign trade and real exchange rate behaviour, 1980–96. *Economic & Political Weekly, 32*(20–21), 1133–1139.

Shah, A. (2013). *Deficit conundrums: The determinants of India's export behaviour* (Doctoral dissertation). Retrieved from https://scholarship.tricolib.brynmawr.edu/bitstream/handle/10066/11353/2013ShahA_thesis.pdf?sequence = 1

Shah, S. A. S., Syed, A. A. S. G., and Shaikh, F. M. (2013). Effects of WTO on the textile industries on developing countries. *Romanian Statistical Review, 61*(6), 60–77.

Sharma, K. (2001). *Export growth in India: Has FDI played a role.* Charles Sturt University, Discussion Paper, 816.

Sharma, M., and Dhiman, R. (2014). Study of post-reform period of Indian exports: A review. *Review of Business & Technology Research, 11*(1), 193–200.

Sharma, M., and Dhiman, R. (2016). Determinants affecting Indian textile exports: A review. *Biz and Bytes, 6*(2), 193–200.

Singh, H. (2010). Workers' participation and productivity. *Productivity, 51*(2), 101–107.

Srinivasan, T. N. (1998). India's export performance: A comparative analysis. In I. J. Ahluwalia and I.M.D. Little (Eds.), *India's economic reforms and development essay for Manmohan Singh.* New Delhi: Oxford University Press.

Srivastava, D. K. (2006). Determinants of competitiveness in Indian public sector companies: An empirical study. *Competitiveness Review, 16*(3–4), 212–222.

Stengg, W. (2001). *The textile and clothing industry in the EU: A survey.* Enterprise Paper, 2.

Stigler, J. G. (1947). Stuart wood and the marginal productivity theory. *The Quarterly Journal of Economics, 61*(4), 640–649.

Subrahmanya, M. B. (2006). Labour productivity, energy intensity and economic performance in small enterprises: A study of brick enterprises cluster in India. *Energy Conversion and Management, 47*(6), 763–777.

Sweidan, O. D. (2013). The effect of exchange rate on exports and imports: The case of Jordan. *The International Trade Journal, 27*(2), 156–172.

Taymaz, E. (2002). *Competitiveness of the Turkish textile and clothing industries.* Washington, DC: The World Bank.

Thor, G. C. (1986). Capital productivity within the firm. *National Productivity Review, 5*(4), 376–381.

Thornhill, D. J. (1988). Barrington prize lecture 1986/1987: The revealed comparative advantage of Irish exports of manufactures 1969–1982. *Journal of the Statistical and Social Inquiry Society of Ireland*, 25(5), 91–146.

Tsang, W. Y., and Au, K. F. (2008). Textile and clothing exports of selected South and Southeast Asian countries. *Journal of Fashion Marketing and Management: An International Journal*, 12(4), 565–578.

Uchikawa, S. (1999). Economic reforms and foreign trade policies: Case study of apparel and machine tools industry. *Economic & Political Weekly*, 34(48), 138–148.

Upadhyay, P., and Roy, G. S. (2016). Impact of exchange rate movement and macroeconomic factors on exports of software and services from India. *Benchmarking: An International Journal*, 23(5), 1193–1206.

USITC. (2001). *Annual report*. Washington, DC: USITC.

Veeramani, C. (2008). Impact of exchange rate appreciation on India's exports. *Economic & Political Weekly*, 43(22), 10–14.

3 Export performance and direction of textile exports

Introduction

In the present chapter, the growth performance of the Indian textile industry and its two groups, i.e. the 'Textiles' group and the 'Textile Products' group, is investigated. The trends in labour and capital productivity, direction, and export performance are presented in this chapter. The present chapter is divided into four sections. Initially, the growth performance of the Indian textile industry and its two groups, 'Textiles' and 'Textile Products,' has been discussed followed by the trends in partial factor (labour and capital) productivity in the industry and its two groups. Later, the export performance and direction of India's textile exports at aggregate and disaggregate levels is also discussed.

The data related to such variables has been published by the various government agencies of India. The data sources used in the book are Ministry of Commerce, Government of India (GoI); Ministry of Textiles, GoI; Directorate General of Commercial Intelligence and Statistics (DGCI&S), Kolkata; Annual Survey of Industries (ASI) (various issues); Economic Survey (various issues); UN Comtrade Database; Central Statistical Organization (CSO), GoI; Database on Indian Economy, Reserve Bank of India (RBI); World Trade Organization; Economic & Political Weekly Research Foundation; World Integrated Trade Solution, and International Monetary Fund. Consequently, data considered for the performance analysis of Indian textile exports is secondary in nature and is based on time-series data collected from published sources.

The data on different aspects of the Indian textile industry and its two groups, the 'Textiles' group and the 'Textile Products,' group like number of factories, gross value added (GVA), number of persons employed, capital stock, and unit labour cost (ULC) were also collected from the data sources in order to reach at a consistent database at the harmonized system (HS) two-digit level.

In order to examine the growth performance of the Indian textile industry, the data was collected at aggregate as well as disaggregate level using the HS code of commodity description at two-digit and four-digit levels.

At the HS two-digit level, there are total 14 commodities from HS 50–63. These commodities are further subdivided into 149 commodities at the HS four-digit level. A description of such commodities at both levels is attached in Appendix 1.1 to 1.14.

This volume takes into account 24 years, i.e. from 1991–92 to 2014–15. Since the economic reforms were conducted in 1991, it was decided to select the period from 1991 onwards. The last year selected is 2014–15 because at the time of analysis, the data was available up to this period only. In order to have a look at the growth performance in terms of a number of factories, number of employees, GVA, capital stock, and export performance, the whole period has been further subdivided into two sub-periods, i.e. period-I from 1991–92 to 2002–03 and period-II from 2003–04 to 2014–15. This division enables us to make comparisons and also helps in generalizing results in more comprehensive manner.

Growth performance of the Indian textile industry and its two groups

The growth of the Indian textile industry and its groups has been examined (see Tables 3.1, 3.2, and 3.3) in terms of various parameters, such as the number of factories, GVA, number of employees, and capital stock for the whole period (1991–92 to 2014–15). In order to generalize the results in a better manner, the whole period has been divided into two sub-periods, i.e. sub-period-I (from 1991–92 to 2002–03) and sub-period-II (from 2003–04 to 2014–15). Average number of employees per factory and employment elasticity is also examined for textile industry and its two groups.

The Indian textile industry

Number of factories

The number of factories in the Indian textile industry increased from 14612 in 1991–92 to 19439 in 1995–96.

After reaching maximum in 1995–96, the number continuously declined till 2001–02 (except 1999–2000). After this period, the number of factories increased to 28599 in 2014–15. However, a small decline is observed in the year 2007–08. The compounded annual growth rate (CAGR) for sub-period-I declined (–0.28 percent). However, it improved for sub-period-II to 6.44 percent. For the whole period, CAGR was 2.11 percent.

Gross value added (GVA)

GVA in the Indian textile industry increased from Rs. 7231 crore in 1991–92 to Rs. 20756 crore in 2000–01. However, a small decline was observed for the years 2001–02 and 2002–03. Thereafter, rise can be seen for the subsequent years and GVA was Rs.83896 crore in 2014–15. The CAGR for

Table 3.1 Growth Performance of Indian Textile Industry

Year	Number of factories	Gross Value Added (Crore Rs.)	Number of Employees (in '000)	Capital Stock (Crore Rs.)
1991–92	14612	7231	1442	8831
1992–93	16856	8223	1512	10594
1993–94	18014	12053	1581	13966
1994–95	18224	14670	1621	17253
1995–96	19439	14656	1826	23078
1996–97	19353	16758	1768	22861
1997–98	19237	17976	1801	25738
1998–99	16518	18045	1610	24472
1999–00	17003	19306	1578	29603
2000–01	16914	20756	1610	27703
2001–02	15830	18135	1491	20448
2002–03	16061	20537	1505	18889
2003–04	16208	21373	1581	19155
2004–05	16796	24597	1703	20513
2005–06	17220	29765	1877	22595
2006–07	18661	37735	2382	31731
2007–08	16449	38259	2085	30607
2008–09	19121	39972	2197	34803
2009–10	19489	48606	2249	39508
2010–11	27810	63471	2323	43805
2011–12	27958	59320	2380	46936
2012–13	27742	77154	2331	49570
2013–14	28170	83038	2474	75793
2014–15	28599	83896	2526	50728

Compounded Annual Growth Rates (in % age)				
1991–92 to 2002–03	−0.28 (−3.04)	8.93 (6.13)*	−0.01 (−0.11)	8.02 (5.53)*
2003–04 to 2014–15	6.44 (7.37)*	13.66 (19.11)*	3.69 (5.53)*	11.50 (9.93)*
1991–92 to 2014–15	2.11 (4.58)*	9.70 (21.57)*	2.30 (7.58)*	6.30 (8.59)*

Note: Figures in parentheses are the *t*-values. *Significant at 5 percent level.
Source: Annual Survey of Industries (Summary Results for Factory Sector), various issues.

sub-period-I was 8.93 percent. However, CAGR improved to 13.66 percent for sub-period-II, and for the whole period, CAGR was 10.17 percent.

Number of employees

The number of employees is an important indicator of the growth of an industry, and it increased from 1442 thousand in 1991–92 to 1826 thousand in 1995–96. Thereafter, slight fluctuations can be observed and the number of employees: 1877 thousand in 2005–06, and the number reached 2526 thousand in 2014–15. The CAGR for sub-period-I was negligible

Table 3.2 Growth Performance of Indian 'Textiles' Group

Year	Number of Factories	Gross Value Added (Crore Rs.)	Number of Employees (in '000)	Capital Stock (Crore Rs.)
1991–92	10840	5993	1264	8149
1992–93	12716	6811	1311	9837
1993–94	12681	9318	1305	12631
1994–95	12447	11370	1300	15264
1995–96	13743	11123	1486	20629
1996–97	13255	13104	1412	20518
1997–98	13824	14390	1431	23115
1998–99	10320	13364	1211	21859
1999–00	10371	13469	1138	25495
2000–01	10031	14372	1108	23475
2001–02	9151	12572	1016	17299
2002–03	9160	14046	996	15708
2003–04	9076	14293	963	15561
2004–05	9135	15616	984	16121
2005–06	9199	19084	1033	17893
2006–07	9524	22173	1101	21952
2007–08	9047	23514	1107	24207
2008–09	9617	21371	1092	25712
2009–10	9874	28868	1111	30156
2010–11	13212	41286	1198	33309
2011–12	13134	34363	1182	35508
2012–13	13120	48665	1153	35539
2013–14	13353	48578	1236	63525
2014–15	13106	46764	1232	37258

Compounded Annual Growth Rates (in % age)

1991–92 to 2002–03	−2.82 (−2.86)	7.02 (4.74)*	−2.52 (−3.17)	7.05 (2.91)*
2003–04 to 2014–15	4.54 (6.38)*	12.61 (11.83)*	2.17 (9.14)*	11.16 (8.28)*
1991–92 to 2014–15	−0.20 (−3.22)	8.31 (15.26)*	−0.72 (−2.21)	5.34 (6.59)*

Source: Same as in Table 3.1.

Note: Figures in parentheses are the *t*-values. *Significant at 5 percent level.

(−0.01%). However, CAGR improved to 3.69 percent for sub-period-II, and for the whole period, CAGR was 2.30 percent.

Capital stock

Capital stock increased from Rs. 8831 crore in 1991–92 to Rs. 29603 crore in 1999–00. Thereafter, downfall can be observed and the capital stock in the industry was Rs. 22595 crore in 2005–06. After this period, fluctuations can be seen for the subsequent years, and capital stock increased to

Table 3.3 Growth Performance of Indian 'Textile Products' Group

Year	Number of Factories	Gross Value Added (Crore Rs.)	Number of Employees (in '000)	Capital Stock (Crore Rs.)
1991–92	3772	1237	178	682
1992–93	4104	1412	201	757
1993–94	5333	2736	276	1335
1994–95	5777	3300	321	1989
1995–96	5696	3534	340	2449
1996–97	6098	3654	356	2343
1997–98	5413	3585	370	2623
1998–99	6198	4682	400	2613
1999–00	6632	5837	440	4108
2000–01	6883	6384	502	4228
2001–02	6679	5563	476	3149
2002–03	6901	6490	509	3181
2003–04	7132	7081	618	3594
2004–05	7661	8981	719	4393
2005–06	8021	10682	844	4702
2006–07	9137	15562	1281	9778
2007–08	7402	14745	978	6400
2008–09	9504	18600	1105	9090
2009–10	9615	19738	1138	9352
2010–11	14598	22185	1125	10496
2011–12	14824	24957	1198	11428
2012–13	14622	28489	1178	14029
2013–14	14817	34460	1238	12268
2014–15	15493	37133	1294	13469

Compounded Annual Growth Rates (in % age)

1991–92 to 2002–03	4.88 (5.93)*	15.08 (7.96)*	9.36 (9.74)*	15.72 (5.92)*
2003–04 to 2014–15	8.42 (7.87)*	15.35 (18.24)*	5.55 (4.45)*	12.51 (7.25)*
1991–92 to 2014–15	5.62 (14.57)*	14.58 (23.33)*	9.00 (19.38)*	12.49 (15.94)*

Source: Same as in Table 3.1.

Note: Figures in parentheses are the *t*-values. *Significant at 5 percent level.

Rs. 75793 crore in 2013–14 and Rs. 50728 crore in 2014–15. The CAGR for sub-period-I was 8.02 percent. However, CAGR improved to 11.50 percent for sub-period-II, and for the entire period, CAGR was 6.30 percent.

The 'Textiles' group

Number of factories

The number of factories in the Indian 'Textiles' group increased from 10840 in 1991–92 to a maximum level of 13824 in 1997–98. After reaching the maximum level, fluctuations can be seen in the subsequent years, and the number declined to 9047 in 2007–08. After this period, the number of factories increased to 13353 in 2013–14, and with a small decline, this number reached 13106 in 2014–15. The CAGR for sub-period-I again declined marginally (–2.82%). However, CAGR improved for sub-period-II to 4.54 percent. The CAGR for the entire period was a concern, as CAGR for the number of factories was negligible.

Gross value added

GVA in Indian 'Textiles' group increased with fluctuations from Rs. 5993 crore in 1991–92 to Rs. 28868 crore in 2009–10. Huge growth in GVA was observed in 2010–11, and GVA was Rs. 41286 crore. Then GVA decreased in 2011–12 to Rs. 34363 crore, and finally, it reached Rs. 46764 crore in 2014–15. The CAGR for sub-period-I was 7.02 percent. However, CAGR improved for sub-period-II to 12.61 percent, and for the entire period, CAGR was 8.31 percent.

Number of employees

The number of employees increased from 1264 thousand in 1991–92 to 1431 thousand in 1997–98. Thereafter, fluctuations can be observed and the number of employees: 984 thousand in 2004–05 and reached 1232 thousand in 2014–15. The CAGR for sub-period-I was very low at –2.52 percent. However, CAGR improved for sub-period-II to 2.17 percent, and for the whole period, CAGR was–0.72 percent.

Capital stock

Capital stock increased from Rs. 8149 crore to Rs.25495 crore in 1999–00. Thereafter, downfall can be observed, and the capital stock in the group was Rs. 15561 crore in 2003–04. After this period, the capital stock was Rs. 35539 crore in 2012–13. The huge rise is seen for 2013–14, and the capital stock was Rs. 63525 crore in this year, and then it decreased to Rs. 37258 crore in 2014–15. The CAGR for sub-period-I was 7.05 percent and improved to 11.16 percent for sub-period-II. For the whole period, CAGR was 5.34 percent.

The 'Textile Products' group

Number of factories

The number of factories in the Indian 'Textile Products' group increased from 3772 in 1991–92 to 6098 in 1996–97. After this, slight downfall is seen for the subsequent year 1997–98, and the number of factories was 5413. After this period, the number of factories increased to 9615 in 2009–10.

Thereafter, a huge rise can be seen, and the number of factories increased and reached the maximum level of 15493 in 2014–15. The CAGR for sub-period-I was 4.88 percent. However, CAGR improved for sub-period-II to 8.42 percent, and for the entire period, it was 5.62 percent.

Gross value added

GVA in the Indian 'Textile Products' group increased from Rs. 1237 crore in 1991–92 to Rs. 6384 crore in 2000–01. However, it declined to Rs.5563 crore in 2001–02. Thereafter, huge growth in GVA is observed from 2002–03 onwards, and it increased from Rs. 6490 crore in 2002–03 to Rs. 37133 crore in 2014–15. The CAGR for sub-period-I was 15.08 percent, and for sub-period-II, it was 15.35 percent. The CAGR for the whole period was 14.58 percent.

Number of employees

The number of employees increased from 178 thousand in 1991–92 to 1281 thousand in 2006–07. Thereafter, fluctuations can be observed, and the number of employees was 1178 thousand in 2012–13, and finally, this number reached 1294 thousand in 2014–15. The CAGR for sub-period-I was 9.36 percent. However, CAGR declined in sub-period-II, and it was 5.55 percent. For the whole period, CAGR was 9 percent.

Capital stock

Capital stock increased from Rs. 682 crore in 1991–92 to Rs. 4228 crore in 2000–01. Thereafter, downfall can be observed, and the capital stock in the 'Textile Products' group was Rs. 3181 crore in 2002–03. After this period, the capital stock was Rs. 9778 crore in 2006–07, and it declined to Rs. 6400 crore in 2007–08. The huge rise is seen for 2008–09, and capital stock was Rs. 9090 crore in this year. Then it increased to Rs. 13469 crore in 2014–15. The CAGR for sub-period-I and sub-period-II was 15.72 percent and 12.51, respectively, and for the whole period, it was 12.49 percent.

Relative growth performance

The growth rates of the Indian textile industry and its two groups, 'Textiles' and 'Textile Products,' are calculated. It becomes clear that performance of the 'Textile Products' group was better in respect of the number of factories, GV, number of employees, and capital stock. To a certain extent, this could be attributed to the fact that the clothing sector was de-reserved from the small-scale industry in the year 2000. Thus, it can be concluded that the 'Textile Products' group was better prepared for the free trade regime than the 'Textiles' group during 1991–2015. Consequently, employment in the textile industry could well turn out to be much more dependent on 'Textile Products' group as compared to the 'Textiles' group in the time to come.

Average number of employees and employment elasticity

The average number of employees in the 'Textiles' group decreased from 117 in 1991–92 to 94 in 2014–15 (see Table 3.4). The CAGR in sub-period-I is 0.30 percent, and the mean of number of employees during the same time is 109. The CAGR in sub-period-II is not impressive, and it declined

Table 3.4 Average Number of Employees per Factory in Indian Textile Industry and Its Groups

Year	'Textiles' Group	'Textile Products' Group	Indian Textile Industry
1991–92	117	47	99
1992–93	103	49	90
1993–94	103	52	88
1994–95	104	56	89
1995–96	108	60	94
1996–97	107	58	91
1997–98	104	68	94
1998–99	117	65	97
1999–00	110	66	93
2000–01	110	73	95
2001–02	111	71	94
2002–03	109	74	94
2003–04	106	87	98
2004–05	108	94	101
2005–06	112	105	109
2006–07	116	140	128
2007–08	122	132	127
2008–09	114	116	115
2009–10	113	118	115
2010–11	91	77	84
2011–12	90	81	85
2012–13	88	81	84
2013–14	93	84	88
2014–15	94	84	88

Compounded Annual Growth Rates (in % age)

Sub-period-I	0.30	4.27	0.27
1991–92 to	(−0.78)	(11.9)*	(−0.84)
2002–03	[109]	[62]	[93]
Sub-period-II	−2.27	−2.64	−2.58
2003–04 to	(−3.15)	(−1.62)	(−2.31)
2014–15	[104]	[100]	[102]
Whole Period	−0.56	3.20	0.19
1991–92 to	(−2.28)	(5.16)*	(−1.60)
2014–15	[106]	[81]	[97]

Source: Based on Tables 3.1, 3.2, and 3.3.

Note: Figures in parentheses () are the *t*-values, [] are Mean values. *Significant at 5 percent level.

marginally (−2.27%), and the mean of number of employees during the same time is 104. CAGR in the entire period was recorded negligible (−0.56%), and the mean of number of employees during the same time is 106. So it can be concluded that 'Textiles' group has not been able to create employment opportunities during the study period.

On the other hand, the average number of employees per factory in the 'Textile Products' group increased from 47 in 1991–92 to the maximum level of 140 in 2006–07. Thereafter, a declining trend is observed, and this declined to 84 in 2014–15. The CAGR in sub-period-I is 4.27 percent, which is relatively improved in comparison to the 'Textiles' group. The mean of number of employees during the same time period is 62. The CAGR in sub-period-II is not remarkable, and it declined to (−2.64%). The mean of number of employees during the same time period is 100. CAGR for the entire period was recorded at 3.20 percent, and the mean of number of employees during the same time is 81. Hence, 'Textile Products' group performed relatively better in terms of creating employment opportunities during the study period.

The average number of employees per factory in the entire textile industry increased from 99 in 1991–92 to the maximum level of 128 in 2006–07. Thereafter, a declining trend is observed, and it declined to 88 in 2014–15. The CAGR in sub-period-I is negligible (0.27%), and the mean of the average number of employees during the same period is 93. The CAGR in sub-period-II is not impressive, and it declined to marginal (−2.58%) and the mean of the average number of employees during the same period is 102. The CAGR for the entire period is recorded at 0.19 percent, and the mean of the average number of employees during the same time is 97.

The findings reveal a small but positive employment elasticity in the Indian textile industry during sub-period-I and whole period as a result of positive employment elasticity in the 'Textile Products' group during the same period (see Table 3.5). However, negative employment elasticity is found in the textile industry during sub-period-II as a result of negative employment elasticity in the 'Textiles' group. This shows a very depressing

Table 3.5 Employment Elasticity (in %) in Indian Textile Industry and Its Groups

Period	'Textiles' Group	'Textile Products' Group	Indian Textile Industry
Sub-period-I (1991–92 to 2002–03)	−0.03	0.53	0.21
Sub-period-II (2003–04 to 2014–15)	−0.57	0.98	−0.04
Whole Period (1991–92 to 2014–15)	−0.38	0.83	0.21

Source: Author's own calculations.

picture of the 'Textiles' group with regard to employment creation. This means that with the increase in the output, there is less need for persons to be employed. The 'Textile Products' group performed fine with regard to employment, as employment elasticity remained above 0.50 throughout sub-period-I, sub-period-II, and the whole period. This group presented a notable show in respect of employment during sub-period-II, as indicated by employment elasticity equal to 0.98. It highlights the labour-intensive character of this group.

The 'Textiles' group presented negative employment elasticities and can be called 'employment-depressing growth,' whereas the 'Textile Products' group showed positive employment elasticities and can be called 'employment-creating growth.' Thus, the net effect on the textile industry as a whole is low, but it shows a positive value of employment elasticity, while during sub-period-I and the whole period, while negative employment elasticity during sub-period-II represented a reduced amount of employment-generating potential of this industry.

Trends in labour and capital productivity

As discussed in the previous chapters, the Indian textile industry is both labour and capital intensive. So it is very important to examine whether labour and capital possess the desired productivity. The growth trends in the labour and capital productivity, as well as capital-to-labour ratio for textile industry and its two groups, are presented in this section.

Calculation of labour and capital productivity

There are three alternatives available to calculate labour productivity (LP): (a) man-hours, (b) number of workers, and (c) number of employees. The present study uses data of a number of employees from various issues of ASI from 1991–92 to 2014–15. Denison (1961) argues against taking man-hours as one of the measures of calculating labour input because the reduction in man-hours per week will lead to an increase in labour input per hour. The shortcoming for man-hours is the unavailability of data, and moreover, the personnel departments may not be in the situation to have authentic data for a number of man-hours (Moon, 1982). It has been argued in previous studies that such employees are much important for getting the work done, and therefore their services must be taken into account instead of man-hours (Kiran, 1998). Due to such shortcomings, several authors have used a total number of employees as labour input to calculate the LP (Palel, Ismail, and Awang, 2016; Velucchi and Viviani, 2011; Klacek and Vopravil, 2008; Subrahmanya, 2006; Hanna, Taylor, and Sullivan, 2005; Nayyar, 1973). The number of employees is a better indicator to calculate labour input. Employees include supervisors, managers, technicians, clerks, and other similar types of employees. At the firm level, LP is defined as the ratio between total product output and total input (Hanna et al., 2005). In the present study, LP is defined as the ratio of GVA to the number of employees. GVA has been taken as an output and number of employees as input. The data related to GVA and number of employees has been extracted from several issues of ASI.

$$\text{Labour Productivity} = \frac{\text{Gross Value Added (GVA)}}{\text{Number of Employees}}$$

The capital productivity explains how well the resources of a business are being used to produce input. Capital productivity can be measured as output divided by capital input (Thor, 1986). The National Productivity Council also examines capital productivity by dividing GVA at constant prices by the estimated fixed capital. So in the present study, capital productivity is calculated as the ratio of GVA to capital stock (at constant prices). Gross fixed capital formation can be used as the measure of examining the capital input. The capital input was measured by subtracting depreciation from the gross fixed capital and deflating the resultant value by the wholesale price index for industrial machinery for textiles. The data related to gross fixed capital and depreciation was extracted from several issues of ASI; the data related to the wholesale price index for industrial machinery for textiles was taken from RBI.

$$\text{Capital Productivity} = \frac{\text{Gross Value Added (GVA)}}{\text{Capital Stock}}$$

The Indian textile industry

The trends in labour and capital productivity, also called partial factor productivity, are examined in this section for the textile industry and its two groups. LP indicates the output produced per unit of labour. It is observed that the labour productivity in the Indian textile industry increased from Rs. 50143 in 1991–92 to Rs. 332131 in 2014–15, indicating an increase of 562.36 percent during the study period (see Table 3.6).

LP experienced an increase of 172.13 percent during sub-period-I and increased by 145.67 percent in sub-period-II. CAGR for sub-period-I was 8.94 percent, and CAGR for sub-period-II was 9.62 percent.

Another index of productivity is capital productivity, which indicates the amount of output produced per unit of capital. It is observed that the capital productivity decreased from Rs. 0.82 in 1991–92 to Rs. 0.65 in 1999–2000. Thereafter, it increased and reached Rs. 1.65 during 2014–15. The increase in the whole period was 101.21 percent. CAGR for sub-period-I was 0.84 percent, and the increase during this period was 33 percent. CAGR for sub-period-II was 1.94 percent, and the increase during this period

Table 3.6 Growth Behaviour of Labour Productivity, Capital Productivity, and Capital–Labour Ratio in Indian Textile Industry

Year	Labour Productivity (in Rs.)	Capital Productivity (in Rs.)	Capital–Labour Ratio (in Rs.)
1991–92	50143	0.82	61241
1992–93	54383	0.78	70066
1993–94	76239	0.86	88336
1994–95	90500	0.85	106434
1995–96	80265	0.64	126386
1996–97	94782	0.73	129304
1997–98	99810	0.70	142909
1998–99	112083	0.74	152000
1999–00	122345	0.65	187598
2000–01	128916	0.75	172068
2001–02	121629	0.89	137143
2002–03	136455	1.09	125508
2003–04	135189	1.12	121157
2004–05	144435	1.20	120452
2005–06	158579	1.32	120378
2006–07	158416	1.19	133212
2007–08	183495	1.25	146796
2008–09	181937	1.15	158411
2009–10	216123	1.23	175669
2010–11	273227	1.45	188571
2011–12	249242	1.26	197210
2012–13	330989	1.56	212656
2013–14	335642	1.10	306358
2014–15	332131	1.65	200823

Compounded Annual Growth Rates (in %)

1991–92 to 2002–03	8.94 (9.21)*	0.84 (0.66)	8.03 (4.40)*
2003–04 to 2014–15	9.62 (14.27)*	1.94 (1.97)*	7.53 (7.34)*
1991–92 to 2014–15	7.68 (22.77)*	3.47 (7.45)*	4.06 (6.19)*

Source: Based on Table 3.1.

Note: Figures in parentheses are the *t*-values. *Significant at 5 percent level.

was 47.32 percent. CAGR for the whole period was 3.47 percent, and the increase during this period was 65.75 percent. Capital–labour ratio indicates capital employed per person. It increased from Rs. 61241 in 1991–92 to Rs. 200823 in 2014–15 with an overall increase of 228 percent. CAGR for sub-period-I was 8.03 percent, and the increase during this period was 105 percent. CAGR for sub-period-II was 7.53 percent. The CAGR for the whole period was 4.06 percent.

Table 3.7 Growth Behaviour of Labour Productivity, Capital Productivity, and Capital–Labour Ratio in 'Textiles' Group

Year	Labour Productivity (in Rs.)	Capital Productivity (in Rs.)	Capital–Labour Ratio (in Rs.)
1991–92	47417	0.74	64470
1992–93	51951	0.69	75034
1993–94	71398	0.74	96789
1994–95	87465	0.74	117415
1995–96	74851	0.54	138822
1996–97	92803	0.64	145312
1997–98	100561	0.62	161530
1998–99	110354	0.61	180504
1999–00	118358	0.53	224033
2000–01	129709	0.61	211868
2001–02	123739	0.73	170266
2002–03	141027	0.89	157711
2003–04	148419	0.92	161589
2004–05	158700	0.97	163831
2005–06	184739	1.07	173214
2006–07	201387	1.01	199382
2007–08	212410	0.97	218672
2008–09	195708	0.83	235458
2009–10	259837	0.96	271431
2010–11	344621	1.24	278038
2011–12	290718	0.97	300406
2012–13	422073	1.37	308231
2013–14	393029	0.76	513956
2014–15	379577	1.26	302419

Compounded Annual Growth Rates (in % age)

1991–92 to 2002–03	9.80 (10.35)*	−0.03 (−.040)	9.83 (5.45)*
2003–04 to 2014–15	10.23 (10.28)*	1.31 (0.88)	8.80 (7.00)*
1991–92 to 2014–15	9.09 (26.54)*	2.81 (5.15)*	6.11 (9.56)*

Source: Based on Table 3.2.

Note: Figures in parentheses are the *t*-values. *Significant at 5 percent level.

The 'Textiles' group

The labour productivity in the 'Textiles' group increased from Rs. 47417 in 1991–92 to Rs. 379577 in 2014–15 (see Table 3.7), indicating an increase of 700 percent during the period under consideration. LP experienced an increase of 197.41 percent during sub-period-I and increased by 155.75 percent in sub-period-II.

CAGR for sub-period-I was 9.80 percent, and for sub-period-II, it was 10.23 percent. CAGR for the whole period was 9.09 percent. In addition to analysing the LP trends, it is equally important to examine the trends in the capital productivity. The results revealed that the capital productivity decreased from Rs. 0.74 in 1991–92 to Rs. 0.53 in 1999–2000. Thereafter, it increased and reached Rs. 1.26 with fluctuations in 2014–15. The increase in the whole period was 70.27 percent. CAGR for sub-period-I declined marginally (–0.03%), and the increase during this period was only 20.27 percent.

CAGR for sub-period-II was 1.31 percent, and the increase during this period was 37 percent. CAGR for the whole period was 2.81 percent. The capital–labour ratio increased from Rs. 64470 in 1991–92 to Rs. 302419 in 2014–15, with an increase of 370 percent. CAGR for sub-period-I was 9.83 percent, and the increase during this period was 145 percent. CAGR for sub-period-II was 8.80 percent, and the increase during this period was 87.15 percent. The CAGR for the whole period was 6.11 percent.

The 'Textile Products' group

The findings of the trends in partial factor productivity and capital–labour ratio are presented in this section. The labour productivity of the 'Textile Products' group increased from Rs. 69501 in 1991–92 to Rs. 286959 in 2014–15. CAGR for sub-period-I was 5.23 percent, while for sub-period-II, it was 9.28 percent. CAGR for the whole period was 5.11 percent. The capital productivity decreased from Rs. 1.81 in 1991–92 to Rs.1.37 in 1997–98. Thereafter, it increased and reached Rs. 2.76 with fluctuations in 2014–15.

CAGR for sub-period-I was again negligible (–0.55%), and CAGR for sub-period-II was and 2.52 percent. CAGR for the whole period was 1.85 percent. The capital–labour ratio increased from Rs.38315 in 1991–92 to Rs.104088 in 2014–15. CAGR for sub-period-I was 5.82 percent, and for sub-period-II, it was 6.59 percent. The CAGR for the whole period was 3.19 percent. The analysis revealed that there was an increase in the labour productivity along with an increase in capital intensity during sub-period-I in the Indian textile industry and its two groups.

Export performance and direction of Indian textile exports

This section examines the performance of textile exports at the disaggregated level, i.e. at HS two-digit and HS four-digit levels. The various commodities at the disaggregated level are attached in the appendices (see Appendices 1.1 to 1.15). To examine the export performance, growth rates were calculated for the whole period (1991–2015) and for two sub-periods, i.e. sub-period-I (1991–2002) and sub-period-II (2003–2015).

Table 3.8 Growth Behaviour of Labour Productivity, Capital Productivity, and Capital–Labour Ratio in 'Textile Products' Group

Year	Labour Productivity (in Rs.)	Capital Productivity (in Rs.)	Capital–Labour Ratio (in Rs.)
1991–92	69501	1.81	38315
1992–93	70249	1.87	37662
1993–94	99128	2.05	48370
1994–95	102795	1.66	61963
1995–96	103927	1.44	72029
1996–97	102632	1.56	65815
1997–98	96904	1.37	70892
1998–99	117038	1.79	65325
1999–00	132656	1.42	93364
2000–01	127167	1.51	84223
2001–02	116872	1.77	66155
2002–03	127509	2.04	62495
2003–04	114574	1.97	58155
2004–05	124911	2.04	61099
2005–06	126562	2.27	55711
2006–07	121482	1.59	76331
2007–08	150766	2.30	65440
2008–09	168329	2.05	82262
2009–10	173447	2.11	82179
2010–11	197200	2.11	93298
2011–12	208320	2.18	95392
2012–13	241839	2.03	119092
2013–14	278348	2.81	99095
2014–15	286959	2.76	104088

Compounded Annual Growth Rates (in % age)

1991–92 to	5.23	–0.55	5.82
2002–03	(5.53)*	(–0.45)	(–3.39)
2003–04 to	9.28	2.52	6.59
2014–15	(17.15)*	(2.36)	(7.84)*
1991–92 to	5.11	1.85	3.19
2014–15	(12.34)*	(4.30)*	(5.56)*

Source: Based on Table 3.3.

Note: Figures in parentheses are the *t*-values. *Significant at 5 percent level.

Product group-wise analysis of India's textile exports (HS 50 to HS 63)

The product group-wise analysis of the performance of India's textile exports at HS two-digit level reveals that total textile exports increased at a compound annual growth rate of 7.85 percent during sub-period-I, 10.22 percent during sub-period-II, and 9.20 percent during the whole period.

In sub-period-I, out of 14 product groups under study, 7 product-groups experienced growth rate higher than the growth rate of total textile exports, i.e. 7.85 percent. The highest growth rate of 21.23 percent has been experienced by 'Fabrics; special woven or tufted fabric, lace, tapestries, embroidery' (HS 58), followed by 'Wadding, felt & nonwovens, special yarns; twine, cordage, etc.' (HS 56) (18.72%), 'Man-Made staple fibres' (HS 55) (14.85%), and 'Apparel and clothing accessories, knitted or crocheted' (HS 61) (12.38%), 'Textiles, made up articles; sets; worn clothing & worn textile articles & rags' (HS 63) (12.21%). The lowest growth rate of 0.68 percent was recorded in the case of 'Carpets and other textile floor coverings' (HS Code 57). The negative growth rate of –7.82 percent has been experienced by 'Knitted or crocheted fabric.' (HS 60), which indicates its poor export performance.

During sub-period-II, eight product groups experienced a growth rate higher than the growth rate of total textile exports, i.e. 10.22 percent. A highest growth rate of 19.20 percent has been experienced by 'Fabric; knitted or crocheted' (HS 60), followed by 'Wadding, felt & nonwovens, special yarns; twine, cordage, etc.' (HS 56) (18.38%), 'Textile fabrics; impregnated, coated or laminated textile fabric' (HS 59) (14.90%), and 'Cotton' (HS 52) (14.03%), 'Manmade staple fibres' (HS 55) (11.20%). The lowest growth rate of 6.89 percent was recorded in case of 'Carpets and other textile floor coverings' (HS Code 57). The negative growth rate of (9.20%) has been experienced by 'Silk' (HS 50), which indicates its poor export performance.

In the entire period 1991–2015, out of 14 product groups under study, 7 product groups experienced growth rates higher than the growth rate of total textile exports, i.e. 9.20 percent. The highest growth rate of 16.61 percent has been experienced by 'Wadding, felt & nonwovens, special yarns; twine, cordage, etc.' (HS 56), followed by 'Manmade staple fibres' (HS 55) (13.42%), 'Manmade filaments; strip and the like of manmade textile materials' (HS 54) (11.87%), and 'Apparel and clothing accessories, knitted or crocheted' (HS 61) (11.7%). The lowest growth rate of 2.15 percent was recorded in case of 'Silk' (HS Code 50).

It must be noted that the lowest growth rate of 0.68 percent was recorded in case of 'Carpets and other textile floor coverings' (HS Code 57) in both sub-periods-I and -II. 'Wadding, felt & nonwovens, special yarns; twine, cordage, etc.' (HS 56) has shown rapid growth during both the sub-periods, which indicates better prospects for the future. 'Silk' (HS 50) showed a significant increase during sub-period-I, but its performance declined in the second sub-period. The commodities which significantly performed better in sub-period-II are 'Wool, fine or coarse animal hair, horsehair yarn and woven fabric' (HS 51), 'Cotton' (HS 52), 'Vegetable textile fibres, paper yarn, woven fabric' (HS 53), 'Manmade filaments' (HS 54), 'Carpets and other textile floor coverings' (HS 57), 'Textile fabrics; impregnated, coated or laminated textile fabric' (HS 59), and 'Fabric; knitted or crocheted' (HS 60). However, the growth performance of 'Fabrics; special woven or tufted fabric, lace, tapestries, embroidery' (HS 58) declined in sub-period-II.

Product-wise analysis of India's textile exports
(HS four-digit level)

After examining the textile commodities at the two-digit level, the next step is the examination at the four-digit level, and it is presented in the following sub-sections.

Silk (HS 50) product group

The analysis of growth performance of 'Silk' indicates that exports of this group increased at a CAGR of only 8.54 percent during sub-period-I as compared to the negative growth rate of –9.19 percent during sub-period-II and at a positive rate of 2.15 percent during the whole period. During sub-period-I, six products experienced growth rates higher than the growth rate of exports of 'Silk' (8.54%). The highest growth rate of 38.65 percent has been experienced by 'silk waste' (HS 5003), followed by 'silk yarn, not spun' (HS 5004) (38.64%) and 'yarn spun from silk waste' (HS 5006) (21.87%). The lowest growth rate of 8.03 percent was experienced by 'woven fabrics of silk' (HS 5007), followed by 'raw silk' (HS 5002).

During sub-period-II, two products experienced growth rates higher than the growth rate of the group (–9.19%). The highest growth rate of 28.80 percent has been experienced by 'silk waste' (HS 5003), followed by 'silk yarn not spun' (HS 5004) (2.47%). A negative growth rate of 21.14 percent was recorded in case of 'silkworm cocoons' (HS 5001), followed by 'raw silk' (HS 5002) (–14.69%), indicating its poor export performance.

During the entire period, four products experienced growth rates higher than the growth rate of the group (2.15%). The highest growth rate of 11.23 percent was noticed by 'yarn spun from silk waste' (HS 5005), while the lowest growth rate, a decline of 10.56 percent, has been experienced by 'silkworm cocoons' (HS 5001). As compared to sub-period-I, the exports of all the seven commodities decreased during sub-period-II, thus holding poor prospects for the future, and hence it can be concluded that the commodities of this group do not meet the requirements of international customers.

Wool, fine or coarse animal hair, horsehair yarn and woven fabric (HS 51) product group

An assessment of the export performance of this group shows that exports of this group experienced a growth rate of 4.14 percent during sub-period-I. However, it improved and achieved a double-digit growth rate of 11.04 percent in sub-period-II. The exports grew at CAGR of 7.06 percent during the whole period. During the 1991–2002 sub-period, out of 13 products considered under this group, eight products experienced growth rates higher than the growth rate of exports of 'Wool, fine or coarse animal hair, horsehair yarn and woven fabric' (4.14%). The highest growth rate (45.92%)

was experienced by 'Wool & animal hair carded and combed' (HS 5105), followed by 'Wool not carded or combed' (HS 5101) (42.23%), 'yarn of carded wool' (HS 5106) (39.1%), 'Yarn of fine animal hair' (HS 5108) (35.38%), and 'Woven fabrics of coarse animal hair' (HS 5113) (31.68%). The lowest growth rate of 2.40 percent was recorded in case of 'Garneted stock of wool or animal hair' (HS 5104). Four products, namely 'fine or coarse animal hair not carded or combed' (HS 5102), 'Yarn of combed wool' (HS 5107), Yarn of wool or fine animal hair' (HS 5109), and 'Woven fabrics of carded wool' (HS 5111), experienced negative growth rate of exports (–14.25%,–0.39%,–9.89%, and –2.75%, respectively).

During the 2003–2015 sub-period, the highest growth rate of 38.34 percent was experienced by 'Waste of wool or of animal hair' (HS 5103), followed by 'Yarn of combed wool' (HS 5107) (15.22%), 'Yarn of carded wool' (HS 5106) (14.20%), and 'Wool & animal hair carded and combed' (HS 5105) (12.60%). Negative or low growth rate in case of eight products (out of 13 products), namely 'Wool not carded or combed' (HS 5101) (–11.53%), 'Garneted stock of wool or animal hair' (HS 5104) (–4.61%), 'Yarn of fine animal hair' (HS 5108) (–47.99%), 'Yarn of wool or fine animal hair' (HS 5109) (–10.12%), 'Yarn of coarse animal hair' (HS 5110) (–15.50%), 'Woven fabrics of carded wool' (HS 5111) (–0.50 percent), 'Woven fabrics of coarse animal hair' (HS 5113) (–7.19%), and 'Fine or coarse animal hair not carded or combed' (HS 5102) (4.59%), led to negligible growth rate of exports of the group during this sub-period. During the whole period, seven products experienced growth rates higher than the growth rate of the group (7.06%). The highest growth rate of 24.41 percent has been experienced by 'Wool & animal hair carded and combed' (HS 5105), followed by 'Waste of wool or of animal hair' (HS 5103) (18.91%), 'Woven fabrics of coarse animal hair' (HS 5113) (16.63%) 'Yarn of carded wool' (HS 5106) (14.70%), 'Yarn of fine animal hair' (HS 5108) (12.34%), and 'Wool not carded or combed' (HS 5101) (8.67%), while negative growth rate of –6.89 percent and –5.55 percent was recorded in case of 'Fine or coarse animal hair not carded or combed' (HS 5102) and 'Yarn of wool or fine animal hair' (HS 5109), respectively. As compared to sub-period-I, there was a rapid increase in the growth rate of exports of only three products, namely 'Fine or coarse animal hair not carded or combed,' 'Waste of wool or of animal hair,' and 'Yarn of combed wool.' However, there was rapid decline in the growth rate of exports of eight products, namely 'Wool not carded or combed,' 'Garneted stock of wool or animal hair,' 'Wool & animal hair carded and combed,' 'Yarn of carded wool,' 'Yarn of fine animal hair,' 'Yarn of coarse animal hair,' 'Woven fabrics of combed wool,' and 'Woven fabrics of coarse animal hair' due to inadequate and outdated processing facilities for growers of specialty fibres, which affects the quality of production, indicating their poor export performance.

The growth rate in sub-period-I improved from 4.14 percent to 11.04 percent in sub-period-II. This indicates that the demand for these commodities has increased in the world market, and the textile industry has been able to deliver the quality products to the end customers.

Cotton (HS 52) product group

An analysis of the export performance of 'Cotton' shows that exports of this group increased from CAGR of 6.42 percent in sub-period-I to the growth rate of only 14.02 percent during sub-period-II, and the exports grew at the rate of 8.68 percent during the whole period. During sub-period-I, out of 12 products considered under this group, only 8 products experienced a growth rate higher than the growth rate of the group (6.42 percent). The highest growth rate of 42.06 percent has been experienced by 'Cotton, carded or combed' (HS 5203), followed by 'Cotton yarn (other than sewing thread), containing less than 85% by weight of cotton, not put up for retail sale' (HS 5206) (19.80%), 'Cotton yarn (other than sewing thread) put up for retail sale' (HS 5207) (16.45%), and 'Cotton sewing thread' (HS 5204) (12.26%). The negative growth rate of exports has been experienced by three products, namely 'Cotton, not carded or combed' (HS 5201), and 'Cotton waste' (HS 5202), 'Woven fabrics of cotton, containing less than 85% by weight of cotton, mixed mainly or solely with manmade fibres, weighing more than 200 g/m2' (HS 5211) with −24.08 percent, −0.72 percent, and −5.10 percent, respectively.

During sub-period-II, the highest growth rate of 34.65 percent has been experienced by 'Cotton waste' (HS 5202), followed by 'Cotton, not carded or combed' (HS 5201) (34.41 percent), and 'Cotton yarn (other than sewing thread), containing 85% or more by weight of cotton, not put up for retail sale' (HS 5205) (17.30%). Negative growth rate of exports is found in case of four products, namely 'Cotton, carded or combed' (−24.35%), 'Cotton sewing thread,' (−3.13%), 'Cotton yarn (not sewing thread) retail packed' (−38.09 %), and 'Woven fabrics of cotton, containing less than 85% by weight of cotton, mixed mainly or solely with manmade fibres, weighing not more than 200 g/m2' (−4.02 %). The CAGR for the product group in sub-period-II increased to 14.02 percent as compared to 6.42 percent in sub-period-I. During the whole period, five products experienced growth rates higher than the group (8.68 percent). The highest growth rate of 22.71 percent has been experienced by 'cotton, not carded or combed,' while the lowest growth rate of 2.01 percent was recorded for HS 5211.

A negative growth rate of exports has been experienced by 'Cotton yarn (not sewing thread) retail packed' (HS 5207) (−11.62%) and 'Woven fabrics of cotton, containing less than 85% by weight of cotton, mixed mainly or solely with manmade fibres, weighing more than 200 g/m2' (HS 5210) (−4.12%).

A comparative analysis of the two sub-periods reveals that six products – namely 'Cotton, not carded or combed' (HS 5201), 'Cotton waste' (HS 5202), 'Cotton yarn (other than sewing thread), containing 85% or more by weight of cotton, not put up for retail sale' (HS 5205), Woven fabrics of cotton, containing 85% or more by weight of cotton, weighing not more than 200 g/m2 (HS 5208), Woven fabrics of cotton, containing less than 85% by weight of cotton, mixed mainly or solely with manmade fibres, weighing more than 200 g/m2' (HS 5211) and 'Other woven fabrics of cotton' (HS 5212) – experienced rapid increase in growth rate of exports during the 2003–2015 sub-period as compared to the 1991–2002 sub-period, whereas six products HS 5203, HS 5204, HS 5206, HS 5207, HS 5209, and HS 5210 experienced a decrease in growth rate of exports during sub-period-II. This may be due to a decline in the export competitiveness as a result of cotton contamination. CAGR in sub-period-II improved from 6.42 percent in sub-period-I to 14.02 percent in sub-period-II.

Vegetable textile fibres, paper yarn & woven fabric of
paper yarn (HS 53) product group

An assessment of the export performance of the group shows that exports of this group experienced a very low growth rate of 1.24 percent during sub-period-I. However, CAGR improved in sub-period-II to 9.83 percent, and for the entire period the CAGR was 6.2 percent. During sub-period-I, the highest growth rate of 85.31 percent was experienced by 'True hemp, raw etc. not spun' (HS 5203), followed by 'Woven fabrics of flax' (HS 5309) (47.60%), 'Woven fabrics of other vegetable textile fibres; woven fabrics of paper yarn' (HS 5311) (45.08%), 'Sisal & other agave text fibers' (HS 5304) (41.47%), and 'Coconut, abacca, ramie etc.' (HS 5305) (34.65%). A negative growth rate of exports of the group during the same sub-period was experienced by three products (out of 11 products), namely (HS 5306) (–9.53%), (HS 5308) (–4.04%), and (HS 5310) (–3.10%). During sub-period-II, the highest growth rate (39.50%) has been experienced by 'Coconut, abacca, ramie etc.' (HS 5305), followed by 'Woven fabrics of vegetable textile fibers' (HS 5311) (37.58%) and 'Woven fabrics of flax' (HS 5309) (34.82%).

Low growth rate of the group during this sub-period was the result of a negative growth rate of exports of three products, namely 'True hemp, raw etc. not spun' (HS 5302) (–13.21 percent), 'Sisal & other agave text fibers' (HS 5304) (–53.02 percent), and 'Yarn of jute & other textile bast fibers' (HS 5307) (–6.85 percent). During the whole period, seven products experienced growth rates higher than the group (6.20%). The highest growth rate of 36.27 percent has been experienced by 'Coconut, abacca, ramie etc.' (HS 5305), followed by 'Woven fabrics of flax' (HS 5309) (34.85%), 'Flax, raw etc. but not spun' (HS 5301) (27.94%) and 'Woven fabrics of vegetable textile fibers' (HS 5311) (21.64%). A negative growth rate has been experienced by 'Sisal & other agave textile fibers' (HS 5304) (–15.45 percent) and 'yarn of vegetable textile fibers' (HS 5308) with –0.94 percent.

Manmade filaments; strip and the like of manmade textile materials (HS 54) product group

An analysis of the export performance of the group reveals that exports of this group increased at a higher rate of 11.05 percent during sub-period-II as compared to the growth rate of 7.94 percent during sub-period-I. Exports grew at a CAGR of 11.86 percent during the whole period. During sub-period-I, out of eight products considered under this group, only four products experienced growth rates higher than the growth rate of the group (7.94 percent). The highest growth rate of 112.22 percent has been experienced by 'Art monofilament of 67 decitex or more' (HS 5405), followed by 'Synthetic monofilament' (HS 5404) (39.5%) and 'Synthetic filament yarn' (HS 5402) (15.82%). The lowest growth rate of 5.30 percent was recorded in case of 'Artificial filament yarn' (HS 5403). Negative growth rate (8.52%) (HS 5401) has been experienced by 'Sewing thread of manmade filaments,' 'Manmade filament yarn' (HS 5406) (–1.36%), and 'Woven fabric of artificial filament yarn' (HS 5408) (–12.11%).

During sub-period-II, only two products, i.e. HS 5401 (12.17%) and HS 5402 (20.93%), experienced growth rates higher than the growth rate of the group (11.05%), while a negative growth rate was experienced by HS 5403 (–1.01%), 'HS 5405 (–50.14%), HS 5406 (–14.75%), and HS 5408 (–3.16%). During the whole period, three products experienced growth rates higher than the group (11.86%).

The highest growth rate of 20.07 percent has been experienced by Synthetic monofilament (HS 5404), followed by 'Synthetic filament yarn' (HS 5402) (17.02%) and 'Woven fabrics of synthetic filament yarn, including woven fabrics obtained from materials of heading 5404' (HS 5407) (12.11%). The lowest growth rate of 2.71 percent was recorded in case of 'Artificial filament yarn' (HS 5403). Three products, namely 'Art monofilament of 67 decitex or more' (HS 5405) (–2.67%), 'Manmade filament yarn' (HS 5406) (–2.27%), and 'Woven fabric of artificial filament yarn' (HS 5408) (–1.88%), experienced a negative growth rate of exports during this period.

Man-made staple fibres (HS 55) product group

An examination of the export performance of HS 55 indicates that exports of this group increased at a higher rate of 14.85 percent during sub-period-I as compared to a growth rate of 11.23 percent during sub-period-II. The exports grew at a CAGR of 13.42 percent during the whole period. During sub-period-I, out of 16 products considered under the group, 6 products experienced growth rates higher than the growth rate of the group (14.85 percent). The highest growth rate of 39.38 percent has been experienced by 'woven fabrics, synthetic staple fib nu 85%' (HS 5512), followed by 'Artificial filament tow' (HS 5502)' (38.36%), 'Woven fabrics of synthetic staple fibers' (HS 5515) (24.82%), and 'Waste of manmade fibers' (HS 5505) (15.60%). A negative growth rate (–15.97%) was experienced by only one commodity, i.e. 'Artificial staple fibres, carded, combed or otherwise processed for spinning' (HS 5507) during this sub-period.

During sub-period-II, seven products (out of 16 products) experienced growth rates higher than the growth rate of the group (11.23%). The highest growth rate of 32.62 percent was experienced by 'Artificial staple fibers not carded, combed' (HS 5504), followed by 'Synthetic staple fibers not carded, combed' (HS 5503) (18.81%), 'Woven fabrics of artificial staple fibers' (HS 5516) (17.45%), and 'Woven fabric, synthetic staple fibre 85 containing less than 85% by weight of such fibres' (HS 5514) (15.26%), while the lowest growth rate of 0.44 percent was recorded in case of 'Sewing thread, manmade staple fiber' (HS 5508). The negative growth rate was recorded for two commodities, HS 5502 and HS 5507. During the whole period, six products experienced growth rates higher than the group (13.42%). The highest growth rate of 27.09 percent has been experienced by HS 5504, while the lowest growth rate of 0.49 percent was recorded in case of 'Synthetic staple fibers, carded, combed' (HS 5506). A negative growth rate (–8.43%) was experienced by HS 5507.

As compared to sub-period-I, only six products gained an increase in growth rate of exports during sub-period-II. On the other hand, ten products experienced a decline in growth rate of exports during sub-period-II, indicating the poor export performance of these products.

Wadding, felt & nonwovens, special yarns, twine, cordage, ropes, cables & articles (HS 56) product group

An analysis of export performance of 'Wadding, felt & nonwovens, special yarns, twine, cordage, ropes, cables & articles' shows that exports of this group increased at a higher growth rate of 20.22 percent during the 2003–2015 sub-period as compared to the growth rate of 18.71 percent during the 1991–2002 sub-period. The exports grew at a compound rate of 16.60 percent during the whole period. During sub-period-I, out of nine products considered under the group, six products experienced growth rates higher than the group (18.71%). The highest growth rate of 34.71 percent has been experienced by 'Rub thread & cord, textile covered, textile yarn' (HS 5604), followed by 'Knotted net of twine etc., fish net' (HS 5608) (32.27%) and 'Felt, impregnated, coated etc. or not' (HS 5602) (31.23%). The lowest growth rate of 16.79 percent was recorded in case of 'Nonwovens, whether or not impregnated etc.' (HS 5603). No product in the group exhibited a negative growth rate of exports, which indicates the relatively better export performance of this group.

During sub-period-II, only three products experienced growth rates higher than the group (20.22%). The highest growth rate of 54.24 percent has been HS 5603, followed by 'Gimp yarn & strip' (HS 5606) (22.66%)

and 'Twine, cordage, rope & cables, coated or not' (HS 5607) (21.23%). The lowest growth rate of 5.17 percent was recorded in case of HS 5604 and no product experienced negative growth rate during this sub-period. During the whole period, four products noticed growth rates higher than the group (16.60 percent), the highest growth rate of 41.04 percent has been experienced by HS 5603, followed by (HS 5608) (23.70%), while the lowest growth rate of 9.20 percent was recorded in case of HS 5604.

As compared to sub-period-I, sub-period-II witnessed an increase in growth rate of exports in case of three products (rapid increase has been in case of 'nonwovens, whether or not impregnated etc.'). There has been a decline in growth rate of exports for six products.

Carpets and other textile floor coverings (HS 57) product group

An examination of the export performance of 'Carpets and Other Textile Floor Coverings' shows that exports of this group grew at a compound annual rate of 0.68 percent during the 1991–2002 sub-period, 6.89 percent during the 2003–2015 sub-period, and at the rate of 5.19 percent during the whole period.

During sub-period-I, out of five products considered under the group, three products experienced growth rates higher than the group (0.68 percent). The highest growth rate of 23.41 percent was experienced by 'Carpets & other textile floor coverings, tufted' (HS 5703), followed by 'Carpets and other textile floor coverings, of felt, not tufted or flocked, whether or not made up' (HS 5704) (3.74 percent), while the lowest growth rate of 1.78 percent was recorded in case of 'Carpets & other textile floor coverings, knotted' (HS 5701). The negative growth rate of 1.53 percent was experienced by 'Carpets & other text floor cover, oven, no tuft' (HS 5702) and 'Other carpets and other textile floor coverings, whether or not made up' (HS 5705) (0.13%). During sub-period-II, four products experienced growth rates higher than the group (6.89 percent). The highest growth rate of 17.31 percent was experienced by HS 5703, followed by (HS 5704) (16.12%) and (HS 5705) (8.75%). A low growth rate was experienced by one commodity (HS 5702) (0.12%). However, no commodity in the group experienced a negative growth rate in exports. During the whole period, the highest growth rate of 31.47 percent has been experienced by HS 5704, while the lowest growth rate of 1.59 percent was recorded in case of HS 5702. As compared to sub-period-I, sub-period-II witnessed an increase in growth rate of exports in case of four products. Only one commodity out of five registered decline in the export growth from 23.41 percent in 1991–2002 to 17.31 percent in 2003–2015, i.e. HS 5703.

Fabrics; special woven or tufted fabric, lace, tapestries, embroidery (HS 58) product group

An examination of the export performance of 'Fabrics; Special woven or tufted fabric, lace, tapestries, embroidery' represents that exports of this group increased at a compound annual rate of 21.23 percent during sub-period-I and at a lower rate of 11.7 percent during sub-period-II. The exports grew at the rate of 10.27 percent during the whole period. During sub-period-I, out of 11 products considered under the group, 4 products experienced growth rates higher than the growth rate of the group (21.23 percent). The highest growth rate of 59.88 percent has been experienced by 'Woven Pille & Chenille fabrics,' followed by 'Gauze' (HS 5803) (32.77%), 'Braids in piece, ornamental trimming in piece etc' (HS 5808) (24.51%) and 'Narrow woven fabrics' (HS 5806) (22.73%), while the lowest growth rate of 2.33 percent was recorded in case of 'Tulles & other net fabrics' (HS 5804). The negative growth rate was experienced by only one product, 'Hand-woven tapestries' (HS 5805) (–8.29%). During sub-period-II, only three products experienced growth rates higher than the group (11.70%). The maximum growth rate of 19.54 percent was experienced by 'Narrow woven fabrics' (HS 5806), followed by 'Woven Pille & Chenille fabrics' (HS 5801) (13.92%) and 'Embroidery in the piece, in strips' (HS 5810) (13.31%), while the lowest growth of 1.52 percent was recorded in case of 'Hand-woven tapestries' (HS 5805). Negative growth rates of –3.76 percent and –7.36 percent was experienced by 'Woven terry fabrics' (HS 5802) and 'Quilted textile products in the piece of one or more layer' (HS 5811), respectively.

During the whole period, the highest growth rate of 21.56 percent was experienced by 'Narrow woven fabrics' (HS 5806), followed by 'Embroidery in the piece, in strips' (HS 5810) (12.11%), while the lowest growth rate of 2.97 percent was recorded in case of 'Hand-woven tapestries' (HS 5805), and negative growth was experienced by only one commodity out of eleven, i.e. 'Woven terry fabrics' (HS 5802) (–1.41%). In comparison to sub-period-I, 'Tulles & other net fabrics' and 'Hand-woven tapestries' experienced an increase in growth rate of exports, while nine products experienced a decline in growth rate of exports, indicating the poor performance of these products.

Impregnated, coated, covered or laminated textile products (HS 59) product group

An analysis of export performance of 'Impregnated, coated, covered or laminated textile products' shows that exports grew at a higher rate of 14.90 percent during the 2003–2015 sub-period as compared to the growth rate of 7.60 percent during the 1991–2002 sub-period, while exports grew at a compound annual rate of 10.95 percent during the whole period. During sub-period-I, out of 11 products considered under the group, 8 products experienced growth rates higher than the group (7.60 percent). The highest growth rate of 45.42 percent has been experienced by 'Textile wall coverings' (HS 5905), followed by 'Textile Products etc. for specific technical uses' (HS 5911) (25.40%), 'Textile fabric, coated etc.' (HS 5907) (23.66%), and 'Rubberized textile fabrics' (HS 5906) (18.62%). A negative growth rate has been experienced by 'Textile wicks for lamps etc. and gas mantles' (HS 5908) (–1.61%) and 'Textile hose piping and similar textile tubing' (HS 5909) (–2.75%).

During sub-period-II, three products experienced growth rates higher than the group (14.90%). The highest growth rate of 21.17 percent was achieved by 'Textile fabrics coat etc.' (HS 5903), followed by 'Textile wicks for lamps etc. and gas mantles' (HS 5908) (20.75%) and 'Textile book covered fabric' (HS 5901) (15.49%), while the lowest growth rate of 1.03 percent was recorded in case of 'Linoleum, floor cover with coat etc. on a text base' (HS 5904) and 'Rubberized textile fabrics.' During the whole period, the highest growth rate of 23.55 percent has been experienced by 'Rubberized textile fabrics,' followed by 'Textile book covered fabric' (19.32%) and 'Textile wall coverings' (18.72%), while a negative growth rate was experienced by HS 5905. As compared to sub-period-I, four products attained an increase in growth rate of exports during sub-period-II. The products were 'Textile book covered fabric,' 'Textile fabrics coat etc.,' 'Textile wicks for lamps etc. and gas mantles,' and 'Textile hose piping and similar textile, but the maximum decline was in case of 'textile wall coverings' (growth rate decreased from 45.42% to –1.48%).

Fabric; knitted or crocheted fabrics (HS 60) product group

An assessment of export performance of 'Knitted or crocheted fabrics,' shows that exports of this group grew at a very low compound annual growth rate of –7.83 percent during the 1991–2002 sub-period and increased to 19.20 percent during the 2003–2015 sub-period, while exports grew at rate of 7.58 percent during the whole period.

During sub-period-I, the negative growth rate of –10.64 percent was experienced by 'Knitted or crocheted fabrics of a width not exceeding 30 cm, containing by weight 5% or more of elastomeric yarn or rubber thread' (HS 6002). This commodity once again showed depressing performance in 2003–2015 (–4.01%). During the whole period, 'Pile fabrics, including long pile fabrics and terry fabrics, knitted or crocheted' showed positive growth (7.60), and 'Knitted/crocheted fabrics' export growth was poor during the whole period (–11.39%). The export growth of 'Pile fabrics incl. long pile fabrics and terry fabrics, knitted or crocheted' declined from 3.83 percent in 1991–2002 to –3.14 percent in 2003–2015.

Apparel and clothing accessories, knitted or crocheted
(HS 61) product group

The export performance of HS 61 increased at a compound annual growth rate of 12.39 percent during the 1991–2002 sub-period, 9.80 percent during the 2003–2015 sub-period, and 11.76 percent during the whole period.

During sub-period-I, out of 17 products considered under the group, 9 products experienced growth rates higher than the group (12.39%). The highest growth rate of 40.47 percent has been experienced by 'Garments, knitted, coated etc.' (HS 6113), followed by 'Men's or boys' overcoats etc.' (HS 6101) (38.48%), 'Gloves, mittens & mitts' (HS 6116) (31.11%), 'T-shirts, singlets, tank tops etc.' (HS 6109) (27.30%) and 'Babies' garments & accessories' (HS 6111) (22.48%), while the lowest growth rate of 0.56 percent has been recorded in case of 'Other garments, knitted or crocheted' (HS 6114). None of the commodities registered a negative growth during this period. During sub-period-II, seven products experienced growth rates higher than the group (9.80%). The highest growth rate of 35.36 percent has been experienced by 'Other garments, knitted or crocheted' (HS 6114), followed by 'Babies' garments & accessories' (HS 611) (17.81%) and 'Women's or girls' suits, ensembles' (HS 6104) (15.56%), while the lowest growth rate of 0.14 percent was recorded in case of 'Track suits, ski-suits & swimwear' (HS 6112).

During the whole period, the highest growth rate of 22.01 percent has been experienced by 'Other garments, knitted or crocheted' (HS 6114), followed by 'Babies' garments & accessories' (HS 6111) (19.55%), 'Gloves, mittens & mitts' (HS 6116) (18.57%), and 'T-shirts, singlets and other vests, knitted or crocheted' (HS 6109) (17.85%), while the lowest growth rate of 1.28 percent was recorded in case of 'Women's or girls' overcoats etc.' (HS 6102).

Apparel and clothing accessories, not knitted or crocheted (HS 62) product group

An assessment of export performance of 'Articles of apparel and clothing accessories, not knitted or crocheted' reveals that exports of this group increased at a growth rate of 6.83 percent during the 1991–2002 sub-period and the growth rate of 8.31 percent during the 2003–2015 sub-period, while exports grew at the rate of 7.11 percent during the whole period. During sub-period-I out of 17 products considered under the group, 11 products experienced growth rates higher than the group (6.83%). The highest growth rate of 29.02 percent has been experienced by 'Babies' garments and clothing accessories.' (HS 6209), followed by 'Brassieres, girdles, garters etc.' (HS 6212) (26.87%), 'Women's or girls' suits, ensembles' (24.51%), and 'Made-up clothing accessories' (16.36%), while the lowest growth rate of 0.33 percent was recorded in case of 'Handkerchiefs.' None of the commodities registered negative growth rate, which indicates the superior export performance of this group.

During sub-period-II, eight products experienced growth rates higher than the group (8.31%). The highest growth rate of 28.63 percent has been experienced by 'Track suits, ski-suits' (HS 6211), followed by 'Brassieres, girdles, garters etc.' (28.36%), 'Gloves, mittens & mitts' (HS 6216) (15.27%), and

'Shawls, scarves, mufflers, mantillas' (HS 6214) (13.07%). The low growth rate during this sub-period was the result of a negative growth rate experienced by three products, namely 'Women's or girls' suits, ensembles' (HS 6201) (–12.91%), 'Women's or girls' overcoats etc.' (HS 6202) (-8.89%), and 'garments of felt etc.' (HS 6210) (–4.49 percent). During the whole period, seven products experienced growth rates higher than the group (7.11 percent). The highest growth rate of 25.68 percent has been experienced by 'bras, girdles, garters etc.,' while the lowest growth rate (0.50 percent) was recorded in case of 'Women's or girls' overcoats etc.' Most of the products (nine products) experienced decrease in growth rate of exports during sub-period-II as compared to sub-period-I. Maximum decline in growth rate has been experienced by 'women's or girls' suits, ensembles' from 24.51 percent during sub-period-I to–12.91 percent during sub-period-II.

Textiles, made up articles; sets; worn clothing
& worn textile articles (HS 63) product group

An examination of the export performance of 'Textiles, made up articles; sets; worn clothing & worn textile articles' reveals that export performance of this group increased at a CAGR of 12.21 percent during sub-period-I, 9.68 percent during sub-period-II, and 11.7 percent during the whole period. During sub-period-I, out of ten products considered under the group, eight products experienced growth rates higher than the group (12.21%). The highest growth rate of 86.24 percent has been experienced by 'Worn clothing & other worn textile articles' (HS 6309), followed by 'Curtains & interior blinds' (HS 6303) (41.34%) and 'Made-up articles of textile materials' (HS 6307) (26.57%), while the lowest growth rate of 9.06 percent was recorded in case of 'Furnishing articles of textile materials' (HS 6304). A negative growth rate of –2.35 percent was recorded for 'Furnishing articles of textile materials' (HS 6305).

During sub-period-II, five products experienced growth rates higher than the group (9.68%). The highest growth rate of 59.74 percent has been experienced by 'Worn clothing & other worn textile articles,' followed by 'Bed linen, table linen, toilet linen' (22.86%) and 'Furnishing articles of textile materials' (22.26%), while the lowest growth rate of 1.31 percent was recorded in case of 'Tarpaulins, sails, awnings, tents.'

During the whole period, six products experienced growth rates higher than the growth rate of the group (11.70%). The highest growth rate of 47.32 percent has been experienced by 'Worn clothing & other worn textile articles,' followed by 'Bed linen, table linen, toilet linen) (30.51%), while the lowest growth rate (8.18%) was recorded in case of 'Furnishing articles of textile materials.' As compared to sub-period-I, only one product experienced an increase in growth rate of exports during sub-period-II, i.e. 'Furnishing articles of textile materials' from –2.35 percent to 22.26 percent.

Direction of India's textile exports at aggregate level

The direction of trade is an important aspect of export performance. The direction of trade depends on the historical evolution of a nation and its commodity composition. Change in commodity composition of a nation may also reflect the change in direction of a country's exports. It is very important to identify the direction of trade as it reflects the export destinations and also highlight the addition of new export markets in the world market. An analysis of the direction of India's textile exports is shown in Table 3.9. It is quite evident from the table that in 1995, the highest share of 23.29 percent of India's textile exports was directed to the United States, followed by Germany (11.12%) and the UK (10.37%). In 2005, the U.S. once again accounted for a highest share of 29.80 percent, followed by the UK (8.62%), Germany (7.19%), and UAE (6.28%). The share of the former USSR decreased from 2.30 percent in 1995 to 0.88 percent in 2005, probably because of the disintegration of the former USSR in 1991, while other countries experienced relatively small variations in shares, which remained almost at the same level. The U.S. still remained the major market for exports in the year 2015, with highest share of 19.08 percent. However, the share declined in comparison to 1995 and 2005, followed by the UAE (9.84%), the UK (6.96%), Sri Lanka (5.36%), and Germany (4.39%), which indicates addition of more export destinations for Indian textile exports.

Regarding structural change in direction of exports, the U.S. witnessed an increase in its share in India's textile exports in 2005 as compared to the share in 1995 (share of the U.S. increased rapidly from 23.29% in 1995 to 29.80% in 2005), while Germany experienced a rapid decrease in share from 11.12 percent in 1995 to 7.19 percent in 2005. This further declined to 4.39 percent in 2015 due to the imposition of stringent environmental and labour standards. Besides the UK, Germany, Japan, China HK SAR, Netherlands, Switzerland, Mauritius, Austria, Switzerland, and Singapore lost importance in India's textile exports, while the UAE, Italy, Sri Lanka, Saudi Arabia, Turkey, China, and Egypt gained importance in exports. It reveals that Indian textile commodities have been able to acquire new export markets in the global market.

Direction of India's textile exports at disaggregate level

An analysis of direction structure in exports of all major product groups (HS Code 50–63) is presented in the following section and highlights that key markets of India's exports varied from product to product. The direction of commodities at the HS two-digit level is presented as follows:

Silk (HS 50) product group

In case of 'Silk' exports, in 1995, the largest export market was the U.S., with 22.53 percent share, followed by the UK (13.47%), Germany (11.76%), the

Table 3.9 Direction of India's Textile Exports at Aggregate Level

Sr. No	Countries	Percentage Shares in India's Textile Exports		
		1995	2005	2015
1	USA	23.29	29.80	19.08
2	UK	10.37	8.62	6.96
3	Germany*	11.12	7.19	4.39
4	Former USSR**	2.30	0.88	0.51
5	UAE	5.11	6.28	9.84
6	Italy	4.58	5.13	4.25
7	Japan	3.72	1.73	2.01
8	Bangladesh	3.93	2.41	5.57
9	Belgium/Luxembourg	2.84	1.90	1.68
10	France	4.88	5.22	2.15
11	Sri Lanka	0.89	1.38	5.36
12	Saudi Arabia	1.24	2.26	2.35
13	Rep. of Korea	1.57	1.59	2.41
14	China HK SAR	2.14	1.09	0.94
15	Turkey	0.92	1.70	2.93
16	Netherlands	3.04	2.47	1.78
17	China	0.34	3.43	6.15
18	Egypt	0.36	1.11	1.96
19	Canada	2.31	2.57	1.86
20	Spain	1.90	3.67	1.60
21	Singapore	1.50	0.66	0.78
22	Yugoslavia	–	–	0.34
23	Czechoslovakia***	0.09	0.15	0.45
24	Indonesia	0.20	0.53	1.50
25	Malaysia	0.62	0.81	1.32
26	Mauritius	1.27	0.54	0.42
27	Austria	0.73	0.23	0.48
28	Switzerland	1.55	0.47	0.47
29	Australia	1.85	0.97	2.00
30	Kuwait	0.40	0.47	0.69
31	Denmark	1.00	1.43	0.68
32	United Rep. of Tanzania	0.24	0.19	0.78
33	Thailand	0.28	0.35	1.09
34	Nigeria	0.35	0.10	2.15
35	Other Asian nations	0.60	0.56	0.68
36	Sweden	1.38	0.97	0.68
37	Norway	0.52	0.36	0.46
38	Greece	0.27	0.50	0.33
39	Kenya	0.30	0.28	0.70
	World	100.00	100.00	100.00

Source: The author.

Note: *Data for Germany prior to 1991 pertains to Former Democratic Republic of Germany. **Former USSR includes 15 countries: Armenia, Azerbaijan, Belarus, Estonia, Georgia, Kazakhstan, Kyrgyzstan, Latvia, Lithuania, Moldova, Russia, Tajikistan, Turkmenistan, Ukraine, & Uzbekistan. ***Czechoslovakia includes Czech Republic and Slovakia.

UAE (6.69%), China HK SAR (6.46%), Singapore (5.57%), Italy (4.61%), and France (4.32%). These eight nations together accounted for 75 percent of textile exports in 1995, about 74 percent in 2005, and around 77 percent in 2015.

The study regarding structural change in direction of exports reveals that only four nations, namely the U.S., Italy, China HK SAR, and Spain, experienced rapid increase in share in 2005 as compared to the share in 1995 (share of the U.S. in exports increased rapidly from 22.53% in 1995 to 29.79% in 2005, and share of China HK SAR increased from 6.46% in 1995 to 9.63% in 2005), while the share of two countries, namely Germany and the UK, experienced rapid decline in the shares (share of Germany decreased rapidly from 11.76% in 1995 to 6.24% in 2005). Apart from Germany and the UK, the UAE and Japan also lost importance in India's 'Silk, Inc. Yarns & Woven Fabrics Thereof' exports, while the U.S., Italy, China HK SAR, and Spain emerged as important markets for exports during the study period.

However, in 2015, the exports in the UK increased from 8.47 percent in 2005 to 14.01 percent in 2015. Other exporting destinations which recorded increase in 2015 as compared to 2005 were the UAE (increased from 5.26% in 2005 to 9.01% in 2015), France (increased from 2.94% in 2005 to 3.05% in 2015), Sri Lanka (increased from 0.17% in 2005 to 2.60% in 2015), the Netherlands (increased from 0.62% in 2005 to 2.0% in 2015), China (increased from 1.43% in 2005 to 13.01% in 2015), and Canada (increased from 1.81% in 2005 to 4.20% in 2015).

Wool, fine or coarse animal hair, horsehair yarn and woven fabric (HS 51) product group

In case of exports of 'Wool & Fine or Coarse Animal Hair, Inc. Yarns & Woven Fabrics Thereof,' the UK was major market in 1995, which accounted for 46.3 percent share. Italy was at second place with 10.17 percent share, followed by Canada (8.83%), Japan (7.73%), Germany (6.18%), the U.S. (3.81%), and the UAE (2.51%). These seven nations accounted for about 85 percent of 'Wool, fine or coarse animal hair, horsehair yarn and woven fabrics' exports in 1995. In 2005, the UK, Germany, Japan, and China HK SAR experienced a rapid decrease, while the U.S. and Italy witnessed a rapid increase in export share (share of the U.S. increased from 3.81% in 1995 to 7.68% in 2005, and share of Italy increased from 10.17% in 1995 to 22.65% in 2005). In 2005, Italy constituted the main market for India's export of 'Wool, fine or coarse animal hair, horsehair yarn and woven fabrics' (with a share of 22.65%), followed by the UK (15.91%), Rep. of Korea (9.07%), and the U.S. (7.68%).

However, in 2015, the exports in the U.S. decreased from 7.68 percent in 2005 to 6.45 percent in 2015 and in the UK decreased from 15.91 percent in 2005 to 14.56 percent in 2015. Other exporting destinations which recorded an increase in 2015 as compared to 2005 were Germany (increased from 2.84% in 2005 to 5.64% in 2015), the former USSR (increased from 0.63% in 2005 to 1.18% in 2015), Japan (increased from 2.28% in 2005 to 10.12% in 2015), Bangladesh (increased from 1.19% in 2005 to 3.02% in 2015), Republic of Korea (increased from 9.07% in 2005 to 10.01% in 2015), and China HK SAR (increased from 0.51% in 2005 to 3.02% in 2015).

Cotton (HS 52) product group

Cotton exports have a more diversified market structure. Main markets for its exports in 1995 included Bangladesh (14.44%), the U.S. (10.66%), the UK (9.50%), China HK SAR (7.0%), and Italy (6.13%). The U.S. experienced rapid decline in its share in 2005 as compared to 1995 (share of the U.S. declined from 10.66% in 1995 to 3.80% in 2005, and share of the UK decreased from 9.5% in 1995 to 1.39% in 2005). In 1995, only three nations, viz. Bangladesh, the U.S., and the UK, continued to serve as principal markets, accounting for 14.44 percent (highest share), 10.66 percent, and 9.50 percent share of exports, respectively. In 2005, China emerged as a new market for exports (share of China increased dramatically from 1.25% in 1995 to 21.57% in 2005), indicating its better prospects for the future. Rep. of Korea also increased its share from 5.21 percent in 1995 to 9.14 percent in 2005. Bangladesh also continued to serve as a principal market, accounting for 12.12 percent share (although there was a decline in share in 2005).

However, in 2015, the major exporting destinations were China (28.01%), followed by Bangladesh (22.31%) and Rep. of Korea (6.02%). Egypt came out as a key destination with 5.87 percent share and Sri Lanka with 3.58 percent share. These five nations accounted for 65 percent of 'Cotton' exports in 2015. The decline was also observed for several nations such as the U.S., Germany, the UK, the former USSR, UAE, Italy, and Japan, indicating reducing demand for textile commodities in these nations.

Vegetable textile fibres, paper yarn & woven fabric of paper yarn (HS 53) product group

In case of exports of this group, the U.S. was the major market in 1995, with 17.34 percent share, and retained its importance in 2005 (the share was 17.49%) and in 2014 the share was 17.02 percent. The UK, which was the second major market in 1995, with 11.27 percent share, experienced a rapid decline in its share (the share decreased to 3.71% in 2005). The share of Belgium-Luxembourg showed wide fluctuations. It experienced a dramatic increase in its share in 2005 (share increased from 7.40% in 1995 to 11.82% in 2005) and a drastic fall in 2015 (with 2.80%).

In 2015, the major exporting destinations were China (22.05%), followed by the U.S. (17.02%) and the Netherlands (8.05%), Rep. of Korea

(6.40%), and the UK with 6.21 percent share. These five nations accounted for 60 percent of 'Vegetable textile fibres, paper yarn & woven fabric of paper yarn' (HS Code 53) product group exports in 2015. The decline was also observed for several nations such as the UAE, Japan, and Saudi Arabia, indicating declining demand for textile commodities in these nations.

Manmade filaments; strip and the like of manmade textile materials (HS 54) product group

In case of exports of 'Man-Made Filaments' in 1995, two countries, the UK and the UAE, continued to serve as principal markets, though there were drastic changes in their shares. These two nations (the UK and the UAE) accounted for 45 percent of exports in 1995. In 2005, the share of the UK decreased to 6.82 percent, while UAE had a maximum share (31.17%). The former USSR, China HK SAR, and Belgium/Luxembourg lost their importance in exports, while Saudi Arabia, Malaysia, and Sri Lanka gained importance in exports. Egypt emerged as a new market in 2005.

In 2015, the major exporting destinations were the UAE (15.68%), followed by Turkey (14.20%) and the U.S. (8.12%), Malaysia (5.14%), and Canada with 4.65 percent share. These five nations accounted for 48 percent of 'Man-Made Filaments, Inc. Yarns & Woven Etc. Product Group' exports in 2015. In comparison to 2005, the decline was also observed for several nations, such as the UK (declined to 4.25%), Germany (declined to 1.10%), the UAE (declined to 15.68%), and Italy (declined to 0.88%), indicating shrinking demand for textile commodities in these nations.

Man-made staple fibres (HS 55) product group

In case of 'Man-Made Staple Fibres,' in 1995, around 43 percent of exports were destined to three nations, namely the UK (16.71%), the UAE (15.11%), and Italy (11.58%). Apart from UK, UAE and Italy, other major markets included Belgium-Luxembourg (8.23%), Spain (6.82%), and Saudi Arabia (5.82%). These six nations together absorbed 64 percent of exports in 1995. In 2005, the UAE (with 19.31%) and Turkey (with 15.38%) constituted the major markets for exports. Other countries whose share increased in 2005 included Bangladesh and Saudi Arabia. The U.S. experienced a rapid increase in its share in 2005 as compared to 1995 (increased from 1.49% in 1995 to 7.38% in 2005). Belgium/Luxembourg and China HK SAR continuously lost their importance in exports. Turkey emerged as new market, having substantial potential for imports of this product, having 15.38 percent share.

In 2015, the major exporting destinations were Bangladesh (14.45 percent), followed by Turkey (11.87%), the UAE (10.35%), the U.S. (7.80%), Egypt (5.86%), Belgium (3.65%), and Italy (3.24%). These seven nations accounted for 57 percent of 'Man-Made staple fibers' exports in 2015. In comparison to 2005, a decline was also observed in 2015 for several nations such as the UK (declined to 2.14%), the UAE (declined to 10.35 %), and Italy (declined to 3.24%) indicating, declining demand for textile commodities in these nations.

Wadding, felt & nonwovens, special yarns, twine, cordage, ropes, cables & articles (HS Code 56) product group

In case of exports of 'Wadding, Felt & Nonwovens, Special Yarns, Twine, Cordage, Ropes, Cables & Articles,' 23.44 percent exports were destined for the UAE in 1995, followed by Japan (13.43%), the U.S. (6.73%), Sri Lanka (6.08%), and Germany (6.00%). Germany experienced a decline in its share to 2.92 percent in 2005, while the share of the U.S. increased rapidly from 6.73 percent in 1995 to 21.60 percent in 2005. Japan, Sri Lanka, Nigeria, and the United Republic of Tanzania continuously lost importance in India's exports. The share of the UAE rapidly decreased in 2005, but still, it remained the second major market for exports. The U.S. and the UK emerged as new markets for 'Wadding, Felt & Nonwovens, Special Yarns, Twine, Cordage, Ropes, Cables & Articles.'

In 2015, the major exporting destinations were the UAE (15.36%) followed by the U.S. (14.4%). Australia also emerged as a new key destination, and the export share was 10.01 percent, the UK (7.01%), Canada (5.02%), and Turkey (4.65%). These six nations accounted for 56 percent of 'Wadding, Felt & Nonwovens, Special Yarns, Twine, Cordage, Ropes, Cables & Articles' exports in 2015. In comparison to 2005, the decline in export share was also observed in 2015 for several nations such as the U.S. (declined to 14.4%), Japan (declined to 1.04%), and Sri Lanka (declined to 2.87%), indicating declining demand for textile commodities in these nations. The percentage share for some countries also increased in 2015 in comparison to 2005, such as Turkey (increased to 4.65%), the Netherlands (increased to 2.14%), China (increased to 2.89%), and Canada (increased to 5.02%).

Carpets and other textile floor coverings (HS 57) product group

In case of 'Carpets and other textile floor coverings,' the U.S. absorbed 34.11 percent of the country's exports in 1995, followed by Germany with 28.99 percent share. These two nations taken together accounted for 63 percent share in 1995 and 64 percent in 2005. There was a rapid decline in the share of Germany in 2005 as compared to 1995 (share decreased to 16.69% from 28.99%) due to imposition of strict environment and labour standards (Kebschull, 1996), while the U.S. experienced rapid increase in its share (share increased to 46.96% from 34.11%) in 2005, which further increased to 48.20 percent in 2015. Thus, the U.S. continued to be the major market throughout the study period, indicating better prospects for the country's exports. The other country which experienced a continuous decline in its share was Japan, whose share decreased from

5.08 percent in 1995 to 1.95 percent in 2005. UK emerged as a new market with 7.55 percent share in 2005.

In 2015, the major exporting destinations were the U.S. (48.20%), followed by Germany (9.44%), the UAE (7.49%), the UK (6.29%), Australia (3.30%), Italy (2.06%), and Bangladesh (2.02%). These seven nations accounted for 79 percent of 'Carpets and other textile floor coverings' exports in 2015. In comparison to 2005, the decline in export share was also observed in 2015 for several nations such as Germany (declined to 9.44%), Italy (declined to 2.06%), and Canada (declined to 1.85%), indicating reducing demand for textile commodities in these nations. The percentage share for some countries also increased in 2015 in comparison to 2005, such as the U.S. (increased to 48.2%), the UAE (increased to 7.49%), Saudi Arabia (increased to 1.10%), and the Netherlands (increased to 2.01%).

Fabrics; special woven or tufted fabric, lace, tapestries, embroidery (HS 58) product group

In case of 'Special woven fabrics, tufted textiles, lace,' the UK and the U.S. were the major export market in 1995, which accounted for 17.5 and 16.89 percent share, respectively, followed by Germany with 13.51 percent share, the UAE (9.22%), and Italy (7.08%). These five nations accounted for 64 percent of exports in 1995. The share of the former USSR decreased to almost zero in 2005. The UAE experienced a continuous decline in its share (share decreased from 9.22% in 1995 to 6.93% in 2005) and further increased to 10.05% in 2015. The share of the UK and Germany declined in 2005 (share of the UK decreased to 8.37%, and share of Germany decreased to 4.05%). Italy emerged as the major market in 2005 with 19.74 percent share (highest share). France and Spain experienced a continuous increase in their shares (though the increase in shares was marginal).

In 2015, Nigeria emerged as the major exporting destination (17.54 percent), followed by Italy (12.47%), the U.S. (10.84%), the UAE (10.05%), the UK (7.24%), Belgium (4.21%), and Germany (4.15%). These seven nations accounted for 66 percent of 'Special Woven Fabrics, Tufted Textiles, Lace' exports in 2015. In comparison to 2005, the decline in export share was also observed in 2015 for several nations such as the U.S. (declined to 10.84%), Italy (declined to 12.47%), and France (declined to 3.41%), indicating reducing demand for textile commodities in these nations. The percentage share for some countries also increased in 2015 in comparison to 2005, such as Bangladesh (increased to 2.78%), Sri Lanka (increased to 3.01%), and Turkey (increased to 2.21%).

Textile fabrics; impregnated, coated or laminated textile fabric (HS 59) product group

In case of 'Impregnated, coated, covered or laminated textile products,' France alone absorbed 13.84 percent of the country's exports in 1995, but it experienced a rapid decline in its share in 1995 and 2005 (share declined to 4.21% in 2005 and 2.02% in 2015). Bangladesh gained importance in India's exports in 2005 and further in 2015. In 1995, France emerged as a new market with 13.84 percent share (highest share), followed by the UK (11.41%), Saudi Arabia (9.63%), the U.S. (8.78%), the UAE (7.84%), and Germany (6.87%). In 2005, the UAE experienced a rapid increase in its share (share increased from 7.84% in 1995 to 15.40% in 2005), followed by the U.S. with 8.78 percent share in 2005, while Saudi Arabia, the UK, Germany, and France experienced a decline in their shares. Japan and Malaysia emerged as new markets for the country's exports in 2005.

In 2015, the U.S. emerged as the major exporting destination (11.1%), followed by the UAE (11.01%), Saudi Arabia (10.65%), China (10.01%), Sri Lanka (6.54%), Japan (5.32%), and Indonesia (4.80%). These seven nations accounted for 60 percent of 'Impregnated, coated, covered or laminated textile products' exports in 2015. In comparison to 2005, the decline in export share was also observed in 2015 for several nations, such as the UAE (declined to 11.01%) and Japan (declined to 5.32%), indicating reducing demand for textile commodities in these nations. The percentage share for some countries also increased in 2015 in comparison to 2005 such as the U.S. (increased to 11.1%), the UK (increased to 3.41%), and Germany (increased to 3.14%).

Fabric; knitted or crocheted (HS 60) product group

In case of exports of 'Knitted or Crocheted Fabrics,' Bangladesh absorbed 34.92 percent of country's exports in 1995 but experienced a rapid decline in its share (share declined to 7.20% in 2005) and then increased to 21.65% in 2015. Opposite to it, the UK, the UAE, and Italy emerged as major markets in 1995 with 19.60 percent share, 12.89 percent, and 11.24 percent share, respectively. In 2005, the U.S. and Sri Lanka experienced a dramatic increase in their shares as compared to 1995 (share of the U.S. increased to 23.24%, and share of Sri Lanka increased to 22.38%). The share of the UK decreased in 2005, but it still remained the major market with 16.81 percent share. Egypt emerged as a new market with 5.39 percent share. Thus, there has been a major shift in the direction of the country's exports of 'Knitted or Crocheted Fabrics.' In 2015, Sri Lanka emerged as the major exporting destination. It absorbed 44.30 percent of country's exports in 2015, followed by the U.S. (22.12%) and Bangladesh (21.65%). These three nations accounted for 88 percent of 'Knitted or Crocheted Fabrics' exports in 2015.

Apparel and clothing accessories, knitted or crocheted (HS 61) product group

In case of 'Articles of apparel & clothing accessories-knitted or crocheted' in 1995, the U.S. alone absorbed 23.34 percent of exports, followed by Germany (12.55%), France (10.75%), the UK (7.83%), and the Netherlands

(6.70%). These five nations accounted for 61 percent of the country's exports. The U.S. still remained the major market in 2005 with 30.83 percent share along with Germany (12.31%), the UK (10.97%), and France (8.56% share). Italy, the UAE, and Spain emerged as new markets for the country's exports, indicating better prospects for future in 2005 as compared to 1995. In 2015, the U.S. and the UAE were the major exporting destinations with 23.05 percent and 20.84 percent, respectively. These two nations alone absorbed 44 percent of country's exports in 2015, followed by the UK (12.5%) and Germany (8.65%).

Apparel and clothing accessories, not knitted or crocheted (HS Code 62) product group

In case of 'Articles of apparel & clothing accessories – not knitted or crocheted,' the U.S. absorbed 36.29 percent of the country's exports in 1995. Apart from the U.S., other major markets included Germany (13.10 percent share), the UK (11.39 percent), France (6.38 percent share), and Japan (4.01% share). These five nations accounted for about 71 percent of the country's exports of 'Articles of apparel & clothing Accessories –not knitted or crocheted' in 1995. Apart from the increased importance of the U.S., the UK, France, the UAE, and Spain emerged as new destinations for country's exports, indicating substantial potential for exports in these nations. The share of Germany decreased rapidly from 13.10 percent in 1995 to 6.03 percent in 2005, and the former USSR lost its importance in the country's exports. In 2015, the U.S. and the UAE were the major exporting destinations with 23.5 percent and 20.65 percent, respectively. These two nations alone absorbed 44 percent of the country's exports in 2015, followed by UK (10.65%) and Germany (7.31%).

Textiles, made up articles; sets; worn clothing & worn textile articles (HS Code 63) product group

In case of 'Made-up Textile Articles etc.' in 1995, the U.S. was the major market, which accounted for 23.16 percent of share. Germany, with 14.67 percent share, was the second, followed by the UK (9.62% share) and the former USSR (9.04% share). These four nations together accounted for 56 percent of exports in 1995. As compared to 1995, the share of the U.S. almost doubled in 2005 (share increased from 23.16% in 1995 to 47.03% in 2005). Other countries with high share included the UK (8.20%), Germany (8.04%), and France (5.71%) in 2005. Spain emerged as a major market for the country's exports in 2005 (share increased rapidly from 0.44% in 1988 to 3.55% in 2005). As compared to 1988, Germany and the former USSR lost importance in India's exports.

In 2015, the U.S. and the UK were the major exporting destinations with 51.02 percent and 7.14 percent, respectively. These two nations alone absorbed 58 percent of the country's exports in 2015, followed by Germany (6.13%) and the UAE (5.65%). Thus, the study of structural changes in direction of product composition of India's textiles exports revealed that the U.S., the UAE, Spain, France, Saudi Arabia, and Belgium/Luxemburg experienced an increase in their shares in most of the categories of textiles exports, while the former USSR, Italy, Japan, the UK, Germany, Australia, and Switzerland experienced decrease in their shares in most of the categories of textile exports. The U.S. and the UAE were found to be emerging as the most important trading partners in India's textile exports. Egypt also gained importance in some categories of textile exports.

Concluding remarks

From the discussion, it can be concluded that the textile commodities of India have made their presence in several international markets. The U.S. was still the key market for exports in the year 2015, with the highest share of 19.08 percent. However, the share declined in comparison to 1995 and 2005, followed by the UAE (9.84 percent share), the UK (6.96 percent), Sri Lanka (5.36 percent share), and Germany (4.39 percent). This reflects the addition of more export destinations for Indian textile exports.

Besides the UK, Germany, Japan, China HK SAR, the Netherlands, Switzerland, Mauritius, Austria, Switzerland, and Singapore lost importance in India's textile exports, while the UAE, Italy, Sri Lanka, Saudi Arabia, Turkey, China, and Egypt gained importance in exports. This reveals that Indian textile commodities have been able to acquire new export markets in the global market. Hence it can be concluded that India's textile exports are diversified to a number of international markets in the post-reform period.

References

Hanna, A. S., Taylor, C. S., and Sullivan, K. T. (2005). Impact of extended overtime on construction labor productivity. *Journal of Construction Engineering and Management, 131*(6), 734–739.

Kebschull, D. (1996). Export promotion of Indian carpets. In B. Bhattacharyya, and L. Sahoo (Eds.), *The Indian carpet industry: Evolving concerns, prospects and strategies* (pp. 42–54). New Delhi: Indian Institute of Foreign Trade.

Kiran, R. (1998). *Dynamics of productivity in Indian manufacturing industries* (Doctoral dissertation). Thapar University, Patiala.

Klacek, J., and Vopravil, J. (2008). Total factor productivity in Czech manufacturing industry–KLEM framework. *Statistika, 5*, 414–428.

Moon, Y. S. (1982). *Labor productivity: A search and confirmation of non-traditional determinants* (Doctoral dissertation). University of Oklahoma, Norman, OK.

Nayyar, D. (1973). An analysis of the stagnation in India's cotton textile exports during the sixties. *Oxford Bulletin of Economic and Statistics, 35*(1), 1–19.

Palel, N., Ismail, R., and Awang, A. (2016). The impacts of foreign labour entry on the labour productivity in the Malaysian manufacturing sector. *Journal of Economic Cooperation and Development, 37*(3), 29–56.

Subrahmanya, M. B. (2006). Labour productivity, energy intensity and economic performance in small enterprises: A study of brick enterprises cluster in India. *Energy Conversion and Management, 47*(6), 763–777.

Thor, G. C. (1986). Capital productivity within the firm. *National Productivity Review, 5*(4), 376–381.

Velucchi, M., and Viviani, A. (2011). Determinants of the Italian labor productivity: A quantile regression approach. *Statistica, 71*(2), 213–238.

4 Determinants of export competitiveness

Introduction

After identifying the variables, the next task is to examine the impact of select variables on export competitiveness (EC). In the present chapter, EC is considered the dependent variable (DV), and labour productivity (LP), capital productivity (CP), unit labour cost (ULC), exchange rate (ER), and real effective exchange rate (REER) are independent variables (IDV). The overview of these selected variables and their relationship with the EC has already been discussed in Chapter 2. The impact of the variables is examined for the Indian textile industry as well as its two groups.

Variables selection

Export competitiveness

Three indicators of EC, i.e. share of India's textile exports in world textile exports, the share of India's textile exports in total exports, and the ratio of India's textile exports to its output, are calculated.

The first indicator, i.e. the ratio of India's textile exports to world's textile exports, reflects how much the Indian textile industry is contributing to the world's textile needs. This ratio is very small in value, i.e. about 3 percent. The share of the industry of a country in world exports may depend upon developments at the international level and rise/fall in production elsewhere. Hence, the indicator may not reflect true competitiveness. Moreover, the ratio being very small in magnitude may not capture the effect of determinants adequately.

The second indicator, i.e. the ratio of India's textile exports to its total exports, may also be not able to reflect the correct competitiveness index, as the total exports includes exports of other commodities also, and hence the relative increase or decrease in exports of other commodities will influence the share of textile exports in total exports.

The third indicator, i.e. the ratio of India's textile exports to its total output, is a relatively better indicator, as it reveals the competence of the nation to export textiles out of its domestic production. This ratio can be increased either by producing more or by reducing our domestic consumption of textiles or by following suitable policies. Because of these features of this indicator, it has been used as an indicator of competitiveness to study the determinants of competitiveness of the Indian textile industry and its groups.

Labour productivity

In the present study, LP is defined as the ratio of gross value added (GVA) to the number of employees. GVA has been taken as an output and number of employees as input. The data related to GVA and number of employees has been extracted from several issues of *Annual Survey of Industries* and has been discussed in the previous chapter in detail.

Capital productivity

Capital productivity is calculated as the ratio of gross value added to capital stock (at constant prices) and has also been discussed in the previous chapter.

Unit labour cost

ULC is measured as the quotient of labour cost per employee to value added per employee. Labour cost was taken as the total of wages and salaries, employer's payment as provident and other funds, and staff welfare expenses. Abraham and Sasikumar (2011) examined labour cost by using salaries, wages, and other labour charges. A study conducted by Tsang and Au (2008) also examined the labour cost from dividing the wages and salaries by the number of employees during the select years. The advantage of taking ULC as a determinant of EC is that it enables the researchers to calculate the influence of variations in the production cost on EC (Ito and Shimizu, 2015).

$$\text{Unit labour cost} = \frac{\text{Labour Cost per Employee}}{\text{Value Added per Employee}}$$

Exchange rate

The Indian textile and clothing industry is an export-oriented industry, so the fluctuations in ER are also important to be considered in the book.

A study conducted by Banik (2008) also indicates that the EC is primarily a function of ER. In this book, the exchange rate of the rupee has been taken in terms of dollars. The data of the exchange rate has been extracted from the database of the Indian economy, Reserve Bank of India (RBI).

Real effective exchange rate

REER is defined as the weighted average value of a currency in comparison to the currencies of key trading partners of a nation adjusted with inflation. The REER is measured as the weighted average of nominal effective exchange rate adjusted by the ratio of domestic price to foreign prices. The data related to REER has been extracted from the database of the Indian economy, RBI.

Quantitative techniques of analysis

The techniques used for the performance analysis in the present book are quantitative in nature. This is supported by the fact that previous studies on productivity growth (Balassa, 1978; Wubneh, 1990; Fayissa, 1996; Hong, 1997) rely upon using standard econometric techniques, such as using the ordinary least square (OLS) as an estimation technique, without investigating the presence of a stochastic trend of non-stationary data. The deficiency and failure of these techniques have been regarded as 'spurious regression,' which is related to the non-stationary behaviour of economic time-series data. Since the regression analysis in this study involves time-series data, so test statistics suggested by Dickey and Fuller (1979) have been used to assess the presence of a stochastic trend in non-stationary data. This ensures correcting the omission and deficiencies in the previous studies of the neo-classical growth model. The co-integration test to examine the long-run relationship between variables, the Granger causality test to examine the direction of causation, the goodness-of-fit test, and compounded annual growth rates (CAGR) are also used in the study and are discussed in the following sub-sections.

Augmented Dickey-Fuller test (ADF)

Owing to the fact that time-series data is used, in order to avoid spurious regression, the series needs to be first examined, whether it is stationary or not. A series is said to be stationary if it is time invariant. The ADF test has been applied in order to examine whether the variables are stationary or not. Stationarity means that the characteristics of the time series do not change over time, and the mean, variance, and auto covariance are all constant. Non-stationarity means that the characteristics change over time.

While examining the ADF test, the null hypothesis (H_0) is that the series has a unit root. The ADF test consists of estimating the following regression:

$$\Delta Y_t = \beta_1 + \beta_2 t + \delta Y_{t-1} + \sum_{i=1}^{m} \alpha_i \Delta Y_{t-1} + \varepsilon_t \qquad (4.1)$$

where Δ is the difference operator, Y_t is vector of time series β_1 and β_2 are the coefficients on a time trend, t is the time trend, ε_t is stationary random error term, and m is the maximum lag length. H_0 is that $\beta = 0$, which means that the series has a unit root. H_0 will be rejected if β is negative and statistically significant.

Johansen and Juselius co-integration test

The long-run relationship between the variables is examined using the Johansen and Juselius co-integration test. Engle and Granger (1987) introduced the concept of co-integration, and it is widely used to examine the long-run behaviour of the time series. This test indicates that the variable under consideration is integrated if differencing is required to make it stationary. In order to make a non-stationary series into a stationary one, the series is differenced d times and such series is said to be integrated of order d, i.e. $I(d)$. Also, if two series X_t and Y_t are found to be integrated of order one, i.e. $I(1)$, then any linear combination of them will also be $I(1)$.

The present study considers the Johansen and Juselius test for examining the co-integration between select variables. This technique of co-integration has modifications over the limitations of Engle and Granger (1987). The Johansen (1988) method, later revised by Johansen and Juselius (1990), permits examining more than one co-integrating vector in the data by calculating maximum likelihood of these vectors. The existence of more than one co-integrating vector means higher stability in the model.

The results of the Johansen and Juselius test gives two test statistics, i.e. trace test and maximum Eigen value test. Trace test is a joint test in which the H_0 states that the number of co-integrating vectors is less than or equal to r (co-integration rank). The maximum Eigen value test conducts separate tests on each Eigen value, and the H_0, in this case, is that the number of co-integrating vector is r against an alternative $r+1$. The equation for estimating the Johansen and Juselius test can be written as follows:

$$Y_t = \prod i Y_{t-1} + \varepsilon_t \qquad (4.2)$$

When the series are integrated of order 1, i.e. $I(1)$, then the system can be formulated in an equilibrium error correction form as,

$$\Delta Y_t = \sum \delta_i \Delta y_{t-1} + \gamma y_{t-1} + \varepsilon_t \qquad (4.3)$$

$i = 1, 2 \ldots p\text{-}1$

where γ is the long-run coefficient matrix, with the assumption that Y_t is $I(1)$, γ cannot be full rank and rank of $\gamma=\gamma<n$, there exists linear combination of y_t. The impact multiplier can be written as

$$\gamma = \alpha\beta' \tag{4.4}$$

where α and β' are (nxr) matrices of rank and r and β' comprises γ co-integrating stationary relations. Then the equation (4.3) can be rewritten as

$$\Delta Y_t = \sum \delta_i \Delta y_{t-1} + \alpha\beta' y_{t-1} + \varepsilon_t \tag{4.5}$$

Johansen and Juselius derived the likelihood ratio test in order to examine the co-integration rank (r) of γ. The H_0 is such that $0 \leq r \leq n$. The cointegrating vector is tested using the trace test as follows:

$$\lambda_{trace}(r) = -T \sum_{i=r+1}^{n} ln(1-\lambda_i) \tag{4.6}$$

Where T is the sample size and λ_i is the ith largest canonical correlation.

Vector error correction model (VECM)

The vector error correction model combines the long-run information with a short-run adjustment mechanism. Once the long-run relationship between the variables is established, the VECM is used to determine the short- and long-run relationship (Engle and Granger, 1987). The vector error correction model estimates the short-run disequilibrium once the co-integrating relationship in the long-run has been established. The rationale behind using the VECM is that there exists a long-run relationship between the variables, but in the shortrun, there can be disequilibrium. Therefore, the error correction model is a measure to bring together the short and long-run behaviour. The VECM allows all the variables in the model to interact with each other and also examines the impact of the variable on itself and on the other variables. The VECM used for the analysis is given by,

$$\Delta Y_t = \theta_o + \sum_{t=1}^{k-1} \theta_i \Delta Y_{t-1} + \alpha\beta' Y_{t-k} + \varepsilon_t \tag{4.7}$$

Here, θ_o is the intercept, and matrix β consists of r co-integrating vector.

Granger causality test

The study uses the Granger causality test to explain the direction of causation between the select variables for the purpose of analysis. The H_0 in case of this test is that X does not Granger cause Y and Y does not Granger cause

X. The findings of this test indicate that X Granger causes Y but Y does not Granger cause X or vice versa. This means that past values of X will enable the researchers to forecast the future values of Y, but the past values of Y will not enable the researcher to forecast the values of X, respectively. In case X causes Y and Y causes X. This refers to feedback effect otherwise refers to uni-directional effects.

Bhattacharya and Mukherjee (2016, p.377) explains the Granger causality test based on the following regressions:

$$Y_t = \beta_o + \sum_{k=1}^{M} \beta_k y_{t-k} + \sum_{i=1}^{N} \alpha_1 x_{t-1} + \mu_t \tag{4.8}$$

$$x_t = \gamma_o + \sum_{k=1}^{M} \delta_k y_{t-k} + \sum_{i=1}^{N} \gamma_1 x_{t-1} + \upsilon_t \tag{4.9}$$

where y_t and x_t are the two variables, u_t and υ_t are mutually uncorrelated error terms, t denotes the time period, and k and l are the numbers of lags. The H_0 is $\alpha_l = 0$ for all l's and $\delta_k = 0$ for all k's versus the alternative hypothesis that $\alpha_l \neq 0$ and $\alpha_l \neq 0$ for at least some l's and k's. If the coefficient α_l is statistically significant but δ_k is not, then x causes y. In the reverse case, y causes x. But if both α_l and δ_k are significant, then causality runs both ways (Bhattacharya and Mukherjee, 2008).

Residual diagnostics test

There are certain properties the residuals of a regression model must satisfy for it to be judged fit for acceptance. The basic conditions are: it must be free from serial correlation, it must be homoskedastic, and residuals must be normally distributed. The tests used to examine these conditions are the Breusch-Godfrey serial correlation LM test, the Breusch-Pagan-Godfrey heteroskedasticity test, and the Jarque–Bera value for normal distribution, and they are discussed as follows:

Breusch-Godfrey serial correlation LM test

The Breusch-Godfrey test is used to examine the serial correlation in the present study. The correlation between time series such as $\mu_1, \mu_2, \ldots, \mu_{10}$ and $\upsilon_2, \upsilon_3, \ldots, \upsilon_{11}$, where μ and υ are two different time series, is called serial correlation. The Breusch-Godfrey test, which is also known as the LM test, proceeds as follows:

Gujarati and Porter (2009) use the two-variable regression model to illustrate the test

$$Y_t = \beta_1 + \beta_2 X_t + \mu_t \tag{4.10}$$

Here, μ_t is the error term and follows the pth order autoregressive, $AR(p)$, scheme as follows:

$$\mu_t = \rho_1 \mu_{t-1} + \rho_2 \mu_{t-2} + ... + \rho_p \mu_{t-p} + \varepsilon_t \tag{4.11}$$

The H_0 to be tested is that, $H_0 : \rho_1 = \rho_2 = ... = \rho_p = 0$. That is, there is no serial correlation of any order.

Breusch-pagan-Godfrey heteroskedasticity test

The Breusch-Pagan-Godfrey test is used to examine the heteroskedasticity in the present study. Gujarati and Porter (2009) confirms that in the case of heteroskedasticity, the variance of the Y population varies with X. This situation is known appropriately as heteroskedasticity, or unequal spread, or variance. In this test, the H_0 to be tested is that the residuals are not heteroskedastic.

To illustrate this test, consider the k-variable linear regression model:

$$Y_i = \beta_1 + \beta_2 X_{2i} + ... + \beta_k X_{ki} + \mu_i \tag{4.12}$$

Assume that the error variance σ_i^2 is described as

$$\sigma_i^2 = f\left(\alpha_1 + \alpha_2 Z_{2i} + ... + \alpha_m Z_{mi}\right) \tag{4.13}$$

Here, σ_i^2 is some function of the non-stochastic variables Z's; some or all of the X's can serve as Z's. Specifically, assume that

$$\sigma_i^2 = \alpha_1 + \alpha_2 Z_{2i} + ... + \alpha_m Z_{mi} \tag{4.14}$$

that is, σ_i^2 is a linear function of the Z's.

If $\alpha_2 = \alpha_3 = ... = \alpha_m = 0$, $\sigma_i^2 = \alpha_1$, which is a constant.

Jarque–Bera (JB) test of normality

The Jarque–Bera (JB) test is used to examine the condition of normality in the residuals. The JB test of normality confirms whether the residuals are normally distributed. It is based on the OLS residuals. In this test, H_0 to be tested is that the residuals are normally distributed. This test first computes the skewness and kurtosis measures of the OLS residuals and uses the following test statistic:

$$JB = n\left[\frac{S^2}{6} + \frac{(K-3)^2}{24}\right] \tag{4.15}$$

where n = sample size, S = skewness coefficient, and K = kurtosis coefficient.

Under the null hypothesis that the residuals are normally distributed, Jarque and Bera showed that the JB statistic follows the chi-square distribution with two degrees of freedom. If the computed *p*-value of the JB statistic in an application is sufficiently low, which will happen if the value of the statistic is very different from 0, one can reject the hypothesis that the residuals are normally distributed. In case the *p*-value is reasonably high, which will happen if the value of the statistic is close to zero, normality assumption will not be rejected.

The Indian textile industry

The share of India's textile exports in its total output, the growth behaviour of select determinants, and empirical results for the textile industry are discussed as follows:

Share of textile industry exports in total output

Table 4.1 shows the ratio of textile exports to the total output of the Indian textile industry. The textile exports have shown an increasing trend in the

Table 4.1 Share of Textile Exports in Total Output of Indian Textile Industry

Year	Total Output (in Rs. Crore)	Textile Exports (in Rs. Crore)	Ratio of Textile Exports to Total Output (in %)
1991–92	34201	11569	33.83
1992–93	40336	15483	38.39
1993–94	50252	18817	37.44
1994–95	63022	23701	37.61
1995–96	74601	28520	38.23
1996–97	76838	33920	44.15
1997–98	94625	36412	38.48
1998–99	86466	40172	46.46
1999–00	98469	45536	46.24
2000–01	107484	54800	50.98
2001–02	96499	51337	53.20
2002–03	106530	60072	56.39
2003–04	114170	62017	54.32
2004–05	134754	63024	46.77
2005–06	156307	77567	49.63
2006–07	198945	86703	43.58
2007–08	199702	89121	44.63
2008–09	225457	96312	42.72
2009–10	261416	106046	40.57
2010–11	348535	126281	36.23
2011–12	372675	159571	42.82
2012–13	400646	198482	49.54
2013–14	497552	250841	50.42
2014–15	483893	258041	53.33

Source: Ministry of Textiles, Government of India & Central Statistical Organisation, Annual Survey of Industries (various issues).

beginning of economic reforms. It reached minimum level (36.23%) in the year 2010–11. Thereafter, it improved to 53.33 percent in 2014–15.

Growth behaviour of export competitiveness and its determinants

Table 4.2 reveals the growth behaviour of determinants of EC of the Indian Textile Industry. The table shows that the ratio of exports of the Indian textile industry to its output increased from 33.83 percent in 1991–92 and attained its maximum level of 56.39 percent in 2002–03, but afterwards, it showed a declining trend and reached 36.23 percent in 2010–11 (with fluctuations in between). Thereafter, an increasing trend can be observed, and the share of textile exports in total output of the Indian textile industry was 53.33 percent in 2014–15.

Table 4.2 Growth Behaviour of Export Competitiveness of Indian Textile Industry and Its Determinants

Years	Export Competitiveness	Labour Productivity (in Rs. Lakh)	Capital Productivity (in Rs.)	Unit Labour Cost (in Rs. Lakh)	Exchange Rate (in Dollars)	Real Effective Exchange Rate
1991–92	33.83	0.50	0.82	0.43	24.47	103.84
1992–93	38.39	0.54	0.78	0.44	30.64	92.1
1993–94	37.44	0.76	0.86	0.33	31.36	100
1994–95	37.61	0.91	0.85	0.30	31.39	103.3
1995–96	38.23	0.80	0.64	0.38	33.44	101
1996–97	44.15	0.95	0.73	0.34	35.49	95.41
1997–98	38.48	1.00	0.70	0.35	37.16	100.4
1998–99	46.46	1.12	0.74	0.34	42.07	94.52
1999–00	46.24	1.22	0.65	0.33	43.33	95.29
2000–01	50.98	1.29	0.75	0.33	45.68	99.3
2001–02	53.20	1.22	0.89	0.37	47.69	100
2002–03	56.39	1.36	1.09	0.34	48.39	98.9
2003–04	54.32	1.35	1.12	0.35	45.95	99.04
2004–05	46.77	1.44	1.20	0.32	44.93	99.68
2005–06	49.63	1.59	1.32	0.30	44.27	102.2
2006–07	43.58	1.58	1.19	0.28	45.24	103.8
2007–08	44.63	1.83	1.25	0.29	40.26	104.6
2008–09	42.72	1.82	1.15	0.31	45.99	103.9
2009–10	40.57	2.16	1.23	0.28	47.44	110.7
2010–11	36.23	2.73	1.45	0.26	45.56	124.5
2011–12	42.82	2.49	1.26	0.31	47.92	121.2
2012–13	49.54	3.31	1.56	0.27	54.4	117.1
2013–14	50.42	3.36	1.10	0.29	60.5	113.7
2014–15	53.33	3.32	1.65	0.27	61.14	111.2

Source: Annual Survey of Industries (Various Issues) & Reserve Bank of India (*Handbook of Statistics on Indian Economy*).

Regarding the factors affecting competitiveness, the table shows that the value of LP increased from Rs. 0.50 lakh in 1991–92 to Rs. 3.32 lakh in 2014–15. The value was maximum in 2013–14 (Rs. 3.36 lakh), which is an indicator of good performance. CP decreased from Rs. 0.82 in 1991–92 to Rs.0.64 in 1995–96. After this period, fluctuations can be seen in the capital productivity and was Rs.1.65 in 2014–15. Unit labour cost (ULC) decreased from Rs. 0.43 lakh in 1991–92 to Rs. 0.27 lakh in 2014–15. The minimum level of Rs. 0.26 lakh ULC was attained in 2010–11. The ER of the rupee in terms of dollars increased from Rs. 24.47 in 1991–92 to Rs. 61.14 in 2014–15, indicating depreciation of the Indian rupee against the dollar. REER has been continuously depreciating, with some fluctuations. Theoretically, with an increase in partial factor (labour and capital) productivity, the EC of a country is also likely to increase. A stronger REER reveals that the home nation is less competitive, while a weak REER indicates that the home nation is more competitive. So depreciation of REER indicates an increase in competitiveness. In case of ULC, competitiveness of exports is likely to increase with a decrease in ULC and vice versa.

Empirical results

ADF test

Table 4.3 shows the results of the ADF test for all the variables used in the analysis at levels as well as at first difference. The number of lags used in the test is determined by Schwartz Bayesian information criterion. In the ADF test, the null hypothesis is that the series is non-stationary or has a unit root (Aung, 2009, p.444). The computed values of test statistics are compared with the critical values, and the probability values are used for rejecting the null hypothesis. If the computed value of the *t*-statistic is more than the critical value and probability values are less than 5 percent, then the null hypothesis is rejected and the variable is assumed to be stationary.

From the results exhibited in Table 4.3, it can be seen that, at levels, all the variables are non-stationary, and they are stationary at first difference. The graphs at level and at first difference also indicate stationarity at first difference (see Figures 4.1 to 4.6).

Optimal lag length selection

After the unit root tests are performed, the next step is to search for the optimum lag length in order to proceed for further analysis in the study. The optimum lag length in the present study is observed using the Akaike Information Criterion (AIC) and Schwarz Information Criterion (SC). Under this method, AIC and SC values of vector autoregressive (VAR) model estimated for various combinations of lag length are used. As quoted in the literature, the lag length corresponding to minimum AIC and SC value is

Table 4.3 Augmented Dickey-Fuller (ADF) Unit Root Test of the Variables for Textile Industry

Variables	At level				At first difference			
	t-Statistic	Critical values at 5%	Prob.*	Result	t-Statistic	Critical values at 5%	Prob.*	Result
Export Competitiveness	−2.154	−3.081	0.001	Non-stationary	−3.859	−3.081	0.043	Stationary
Labour Productivity	1.903	−3.029	0.999	Non-stationary	−3.288	−3.020	0.004	Stationary
Capital Productivity	−0.232	−3.004	0.920	Non-stationary	−9.655	−3.00	0.000	Stationary
Unit Labour Cost	−2.741	−2.998	0.082	Non-stationary	−6.374	−3.004	0.000	Stationary
Exchange Rate	−0.917	−2.998	0.764	Non-stationary	−4.427	−3.004	0.002	Stationary
Real Effective Exchange Rate	−1.372	−2.998	0.577	Non-stationary	−5.478	−3.004	0.000	Stationary

Source: The author.

EC

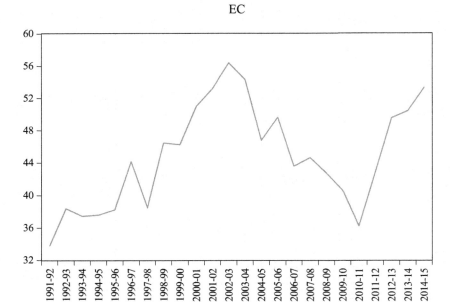

Figure 4.1(a) Export Competitiveness (Level) (Textile Industry)

DIFEC

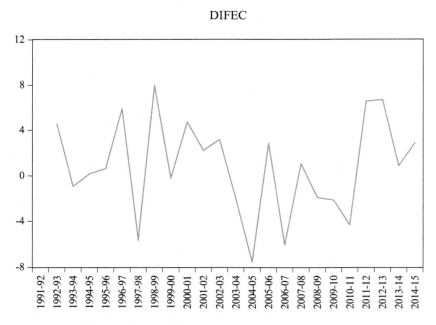

Figure 4.1(b) Export Competitiveness (First Difference)

(LP)

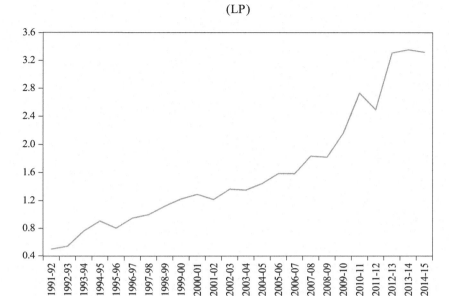

Figure 4.2(a) Labour Productivity (Level)

DIFLP

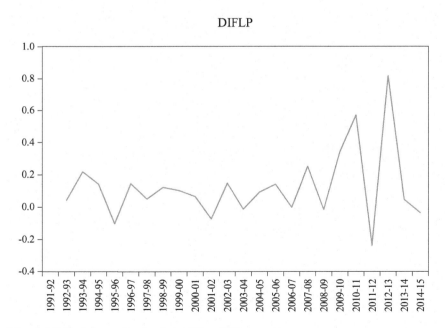

Figure 4.2(b) Labour Productivity (First Difference)

(CP)

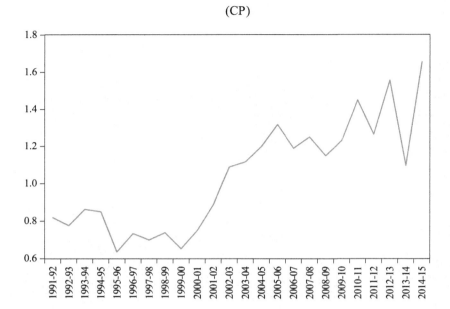

Figure 4.3(a) Capital Productivity (Level)

DIFCP

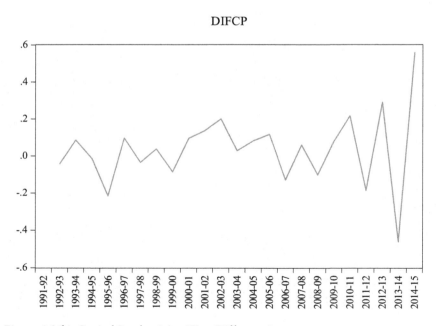

Figure 4.3(b) Capital Productivity (First Difference)

(ULC)

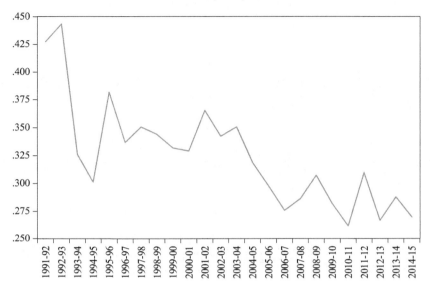

Figure 4.4(a) Unit Labour Cost (Level)

DIFULC

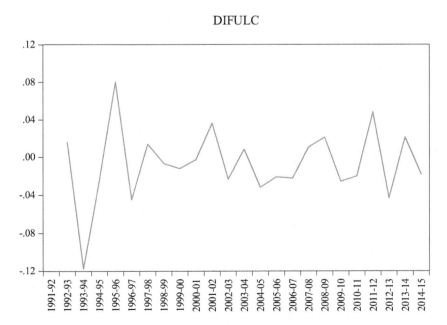

Figure 4.4(b) Unit Labour Cost (First Difference)

(ER)

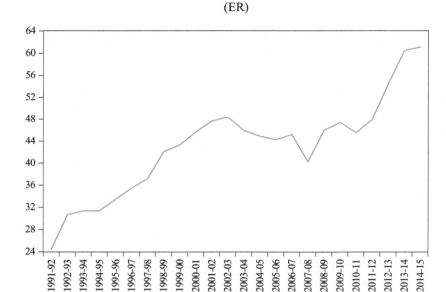

Figure 4.5(a) Exchange Rate (Level)

DIFER

Figure 4.5 (b) Exchange Rate (First Difference)

(REER)

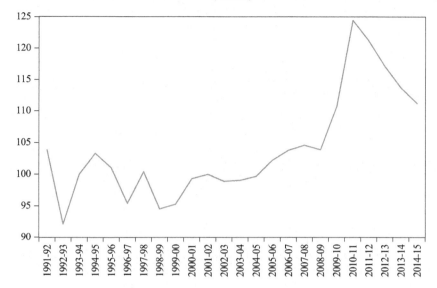

Figure 4.6(a) Real Effective Exchange Rate (Level)

DIFREER

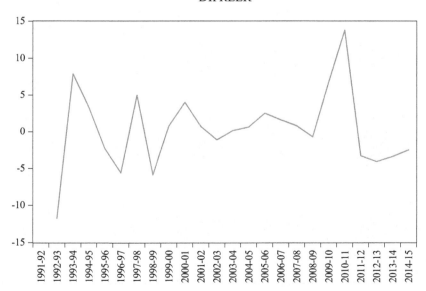

Figure 4.6(b) Real Effective Exchange Rate (First Difference)

Source: On the basis of data compiled and generated on EViews software by author.

the optimum lag length (Aung, 2009, p. 327). However, in case any clash emerges between the AIC and SC, one must decide the optimum lag length based on SC criteria. In the present study, no such controversy emerges, and the values of AIC and SC are minimum, i.e. 4.775 and 8.643, respectively, for lag length two. Hence, two lags for the further analysis can be selected.

Granger causality test

Correlation does not reveal any causation in the meaningful sense. So in the present study, the Granger causality test is estimated in order to examine the direction of causality between the EC and other variables. The null hypotheses of the Granger causality test is that x does not Granger cause y and y does not Granger cause x. The findings of this test are given in Table 4.4 and show the presence of only uni-directional causality running from LP, CP, ULC, ER, and REER to EC. The variables are defined as EC – export competitiveness, LP – labour productivity, CP – capital productivity, ULC – unit labour cost, ER – exchange rate, and REER –real effective exchange rate.

The results of the present study show the absence of feedback effects or bi-directional effects among the variables, and only uni-directional causality is found, which indicates that the selected variables have effects on the EC of

Table 4.4 Granger Causality Test (Textile Industry)

Null Hypothesis	F-Statistic	Prob*	Results	Direction
LP does not Granger Cause EC	3.865	0.042	C	Uni-directional
EC does not Granger Cause LP	0.117	0.890	NC	
CP does not Granger Cause EC	1.364	0.032	C	Uni-directional
EC does not Granger Cause CP	0.031	0.969	NC	
ULC does not Granger Cause EC	2.657	0.047	C	Uni-directional
EC does not Granger Cause ULC	0.522	0.602	NC	
ER does not Granger Cause EC	5.516	0.013	C	Uni-directional
EC does not Granger Cause ER	1.012	0.446	NC	
REER does not Granger Cause EC	2.987	0.041	C	Uni-directional
EC does not Granger Cause REER	1.296	0.307	NC	

Source: Author's own calculations.

* Significant at 5 percent level.
C stands for 'Causality' and NC for 'No Causality.'

the textile industry. These results also confirm the earlier studies conducted by De Grauwe and Verfaille (1988); Broll and Eckwert (1999).

Johansen and Juselius co-integration test

The Johansen and Juselius co-integration test is used to test the existence of a long-run relationship between the select variables. Since the variables are non-stationary at the level and all the variables are integrated of the same order at first difference, i.e. $I(1)$, the co-integration test can be applied. The variables at level (non-stationary) are used for the purpose of analysis for testing the co-integration. Tables 4.5 and 4.6 highlight the findings of trace and maximum Eigen value statistics from which the number of co-integrated equations or long relationship between the variable can be examined for the Indian textile industry.

Table 4.5 Johansen and Juselius Co-integration Test: Trace Statistics

Testing the Existence and No. of Co-integration Relationships

Hypothesis (No. of Co-integration Equations)	*Trace Statistics*	*0.05 Critical Value*	*Prob.*
None	216.361	95.753	0.000
At most 1	135.932	69.818	0.000
At most 2	84.637	47.856	0.000
At most 3	45.813	29.797	0.000
At most 4	22.813	15.494	0.003
At most 5	9.189	3.841	0.002

Source: Author's own calculations.

Table 4.6 Johansen and Juselius Co-integration Test: Max Eigen Statistics

Testing the Existence and No. of Co-integration Relationships

Hypothesis (No. of Co-integration Equations)	*Max Eigen value*	*0.05 Critical Value*	*Prob.*
None	80.429	40.077	0.000
At most 1	51.295	33.876	0.000
At most 2	38.823	27.584	0.001
At most 3	23.000	21.131	0.027
At most 4	13.623	14.264	0.062
At most 5	9.189	3.841	0.002

Source: Author's own calculations.

Table 4.7 Regression Results

R-squared	Adjusted R-squared	F-statistic	Prob. (F-statistic)
0.840	0.795	18.929	0.000

Source: Author's own calculations.

The null hypothesis is rejected when the estimated value of trace statistics and maximum Eigen value statistics is more than the critical values at 5 percent significance level (Prakash, Nauriyal, and Kaur, 2017). The findings of the test reveal that the trace statistics have six co-integrating equations at 5 percent level, and maximum Eigen value statistics have four co-integrated equations in the model, which reveals the long-run relationship between the select variables for the Indian textile industry. These findings are supported by Grossman and Helpman (1991); Rivera-Batiz and Romer (1991).

From Table 4.7, it is clear that the values of R-squared and adjusted R-squared in the model are 0.840 and 0.795, respectively. This indicates that all the variables such as LP, CP, ULC, ER and REER have a significant influence on the EC of the Indian textile industry. Similar findings were given by Kumar and Siddharthan (1994); Kordalska and Olczyk (2014).

Results of vector error correction model

After the co-integration relationship has been established in the longrun, the next step is the estimation of short-run disequilibrium. The vector error correction (VEC) model is a restricted VAR designed for use with non-stationary series that are known to be co-integrated. From the results of the co-integration test, it is very clear that the variables are co-integrated in the long-run, so the vector error correction model (VECM) can be applied. It must be noted that in case of the VECM, the variables or series must be stationary. It means that the variables must be taken on the first difference (Khatun, 2016). In the VECM, the error correction terms are estimated for both the short-run and long-run in the textile industry. As per literature, the long-run coefficients or error correction terms must be negative and significant (Khatun, 2016; Prakash et al., 2017). The results of the VECM are presented in Table 4.8 and reveal that the long-run coefficient of co-integrating model C(1) is negative but not significant. Hence, there is no long-run causality running from (IVs), i.e. LP, CP, ULC, ER, and REER to the DV, i.e. EC. These findings also support Fang, Lai, and Miller (2004); Kordalska and Olczyk (2014). The ECM model generated is as follows:

D (DIFEC) = C(1)* (DIFEC(−1) + 7.9357* DIFER (−1) + 4.7541* DIFREER (1) 16.7467) + C(2)* (DIFLP (−1) −0.1948* DIFER (−1) 0.1176* DIFREER(−1) + 0.2642) + C(3)* (DIFCP (−1) 0.4720

*DIFER (–1)–0.2433*DIFREER (–1) + 0.9063) + C(4)* (DIFULC(–1) + 0.0538*DIFER (–1) + 0.0252* DIFREER (–1) –0.0950) + C(5)*D(DIFEC (–1)) + C(6)* D(DIFLP (–1)) + C(7)* D(DIFCP (–1)) + C(8)* D(DIFULC(–1)) + C(9)*D(DIFER (–1)) + C(10) *D(DIFREER (–1)) + C(11)

where C(1) is the coefficient of co-integrating model or error correction term in the longrun, C(11) is constant, and C(2) to C(10) are short-run coefficients.

After estimating the long-run causality from IVs to DV, now the short-run causality running from IVs to DV is examined. The Wald test to check the short-run causality has been conducted. Table 4.9 presents Chi-square test statistics to test the null hypothesis that the cause variables do not affect the effect variable along with the *p*-values. From the table, it can be inferred that Chi-square test statistics are non-significant at 5 percent level of significance. Hence the null hypothesis is accepted that there is no short-run causality running from IVs to DV. The summary of the model is that there is no long-run or short-run causality running from IVs to DV.

The null hypothesis of the Wald test is:

C(2) = C(6) = 0; C(3) = C(7) = 0; C(4) = C(8) = 0; C(9) = 0; C(10) = 0

Diagnostic test

After the VECM tests are performed, the next step is to check how the model is as a whole. For this purpose, the diagnostic tests are performed. The regression result indicated high R-squared value (0.685), which is quite

Table 4.8 Result of the Error Correction Model

Variable	Coefficient	Probability
C(1)	–0.466	0.406
C(2)	–1.735	0.906
C(3)	–13.858	0.274
C(4)	–43.883	0.470
C(5)	–0.618	0.146
C(6)	–6.269	0.705
C(7)	22.319	0.331
C(8)	61.183	0.105
C(9)	–0.318	0.611
C(10)	–0.233	0.569
C(11)	0.597	0.644

Source: Author's own calculations.

R-squared = 0.685.

Table 4.9 Short-Run Causality
(Wald Test)

Variables	Probability
LP	0.645
CP	0.484
ULC	0.185
ER	0.600
REER	0.556

Source: Author's own calculations.

Table 4.10 Diagnostic Test

Test	Null Hypotheses	Value
Normality Test (Jarque–Bera Statistic)	Null Hypotheses: Residuals are normally distributed	1.923 (0.382)
Serial Correlation (Breusch-Godfrey Serial Correlation LM Test)	Null Hypotheses: Residuals are not serially correlated	0.033 (0.940)
Heteroskedasticity Test (Breusch-Pagan-Godfrey)	Null Hypotheses: Residuals are not heteroskedastic	0.512 (0.708)

Source: Author's own calculations.

Note: Values in parentheses " ()"indicate the *p*-value.

high. So the model can be accepted, and further diagnostic tests are performed. Table 4.10 displays the results of the diagnostic test for the VECM, which suggest that the model is normally distributed with a probability of Jarque–Bera statistics more than 5 percent. The model also does not suffer from the problems of serial correlation and heteroskedasticity. The probability values of F-statistic of the Breusch-Godfrey serial correlation LM test and the Breusch-Pagan-Godfrey test are more than 5 percent, so the null hypothesis is not rejected for the Indian textile industry. This reveals that the model has the property of goodness of fit.

The 'Textiles' group

The share of India's 'Textiles' group exports in its total output, the growth behaviour of select determinants, and empirical results are presented in this section.

Share of 'Textiles' exports in total output

Table 4.11 shows the ratio of textile exports to the total output of the Indian 'Textiles' group. It is seen that this ratio increased from 32.70 percent in 1991–92 and reached 50.14 percent in 2002–03. Thereafter, slight fluctuations can

Table 4.11 Share of 'Textile' Exports in Total Output of Indian 'Textiles' Group

Year	Total Output (in Rs. Crore)	Textile Exports (in Rs. Crore)	Ratio of Textile Exports to Total Output (in %)
1991–92	28857	8952	32.70
1992–93	33909	12680	39.74
1993–94	40657	15517	33.87
1994–95	50916	20085	34.72
1995–96	59513	24353	35.46
1996–97	61910	29367	41.04
1997–98	76858	31481	34.96
1998–99	65884	34323	43.56
1999–00	71522	39099	43.68
2000–01	77035	48209	47.58
2001–02	70601	45379	49.97
2002–03	73611	52431	50.14
2003–04	79004	55559	46.89
2004–05	88912	56753	46.56
2005–06	102207	69846	47.82
2006–07	117928	78683	48.31
2007–08	134024	81313	49.78
2008–09	135891	89306	50.36
2009–10	162083	98451	51.26
2010–11	233082	115999	53.33
2011–12	247030	148534	52.37
2012–13	264223	184628	53.32
2013–14	317180	236705	53.67
2014–15	318140	243243	54.63

Source: The author.

be seen till 2007–08, and the share was 49.78 percent. Thereafter, an increasing trend can be observed, and the share of textile exports in total output of the Indian 'Textiles' group was 54.63 percent in 2014–15.

Growth behaviour of export competitiveness and its determinants

Table 4.12 reveals the growth behaviour of determinants of EC of the Indian 'Textiles' group. The table shows that the ratio of exports of the Indian 'Textiles' group to its output increased from 32.70 percent in 1991–92 and attained its maximum level of 54.63 percent in 2014–15 (with some fluctuations).

Regarding the factors affecting competitiveness, the table shows that the value of labour productivity increased from Rs. 0.47 lakh in 1991–92 to Rs. 3.80 lakh in 2014–15. The value was maximum in 2012–13 (Rs. 4.22 lakh). Capital productivity decreased from Rs. 0.74 in 1991–92 to Rs. 0.53 in 1999–00. After this period, fluctuations can be seen in the capital productivity, and it was Rs.1.26 in 2014–15. ULC decreased from Rs. 0.47 lakh in 1991–92 to Rs. 0.25 lakh in 2014–15. The minimum level of Rs. 0.22 lakh ULC was attained twice in 2010–11 and 2012–13. The exchange rate of the rupee in terms of dollars increased from Rs. 24.47 in 1991–92 to Rs. 61.14

Table 4.12 Growth Behaviour of Export Competitiveness of 'Textiles' Group and Its Determinants

Years	Export Competitiveness	Labour Productivity (in Rs. Lakh)	Capital Productivity (in Rs.)	Unit Labour Cost (Rs. Lakh)	Exchange Rate (in Dollars)	Real Effective Exchange Rate
1991–92	32.70	0.47	0.74	0.47	24.47	103.84
1992–93	39.74	0.52	0.69	0.49	30.64	92.1
1993–94	33.87	0.71	0.74	0.37	31.36	100
1994–95	34.72	0.87	0.74	0.34	31.39	103.3
1995–96	35.46	0.75	0.54	0.44	33.44	101
1996–97	41.04	0.93	0.64	0.37	35.49	95.41
1997–98	34.96	1.01	0.62	0.37	37.16	100.4
1998–99	43.56	1.10	0.61	0.39	42.07	94.52
1999–00	43.68	1.18	0.53	0.38	43.33	95.29
2000–01	47.58	1.30	0.61	0.37	45.68	99.3
2001–02	49.97	1.24	0.73	0.40	47.69	100
2002–03	50.14	1.41	0.89	0.37	48.39	98.9
2003–04	46.89	1.48	0.92	0.37	45.95	99.04
2004–05	46.56	1.59	0.97	0.33	44.93	99.68
2005–06	47.82	1.85	1.07	0.29	44.27	102.2
2006–07	48.31	2.01	1.01	0.27	45.24	103.8
2007–08	49.78	2.12	0.97	0.27	40.26	104.6
2008–09	50.36	1.96	0.83	0.30	45.99	103.9
2009–10	51.26	2.60	0.96	0.25	47.44	110.7
2010–11	53.33	3.45	1.24	0.22	45.56	124.5
2011–12	52.37	2.91	0.97	0.28	47.92	121.2
2012–13	53.32	4.22	1.37	0.22	54.4	117.1
2013–14	53.67	3.93	0.76	0.26	60.5	113.7
2014–15	54.63	3.80	1.26	0.25	61.14	111.2

Source: The author.

in 2014–15, indicating depreciation of the Indian rupee against the dollar. REER has been continuously depreciating with some fluctuations.

Empirical results

The empirical results of various techniques of analysis are presented in this section for the Indian 'Textiles' group.

ADF test

Table 4.13 shows the results of the ADF test for all the variables used in the analysis at levels as well as at first difference. The number of lags used in the test is determined by the Schwartz Bayesian information criterion. From the results exhibited in Table 4.13, it can be seen that, at levels, all the variables are non-stationary, and they are stationary at first difference. The graphs of stationarity (see Figures 4.7 to 4.12) are also presented for each variable at the level and the first difference for the 'Textiles' group.

Table 4.13 Augmented Dickey-Fuller (ADF) Unit Root Test of the Variables for 'Textiles' Group

Variables	At level				At first difference			
	t-Statistic	Critical values at 5%	Prob.*	Result	t-Statistic	Critical values at 5%	Prob.*	Result
Export Competitiveness	-1.609	-2.998	0.461	Non-stationary	-8.860	-3.004	0.000	Stationary
Labour Productivity	1.840	-3.081	0.999	Non-stationary	-4.042	-3.081	0.031	Stationary
Capital Productivity	-0.821	-3.00	0.793	Non-stationary	-10.695	-3.004	0.000	Stationary
Unit Labour Cost	-2.039	-3.004	0.269	Non-stationary	-6.831	-3.00	0.000	Stationary
Exchange Rate	-0.917	-2.998	0.764	Non-stationary	-4.427	-3.004	0.002	Stationary
Real Effective Exchange Rate	-1.372	-2.998	0.577	Non-stationary	-5.478	-3.00	0.000	Stationary

Source: The author.

EC

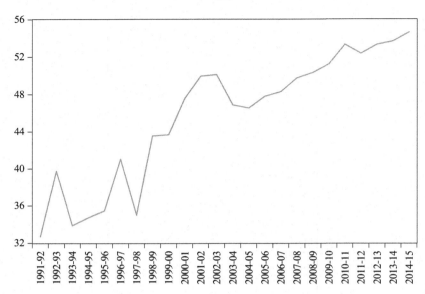

Figure 4.7(a) Export Competitiveness (Level) (Textile Industry)

DIFEC

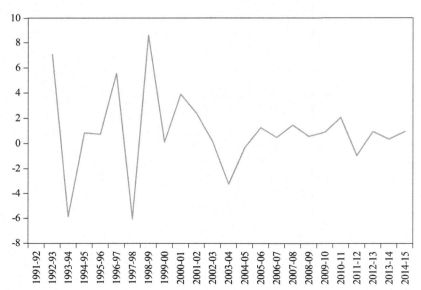

Figure 4.7(b) Export Competitiveness (First Difference)

(LP)

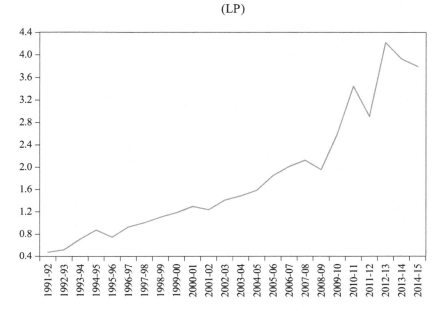

Figure 4.8(a) Labour Productivity (Level)

DIFLP

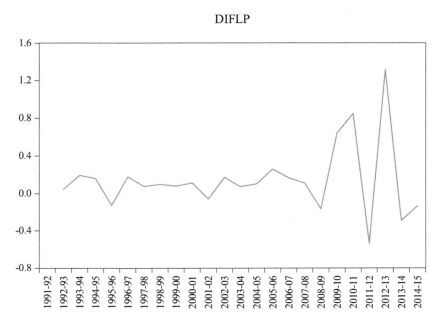

Figure 4.8(b) Labour Productivity (First Difference)

(CP)

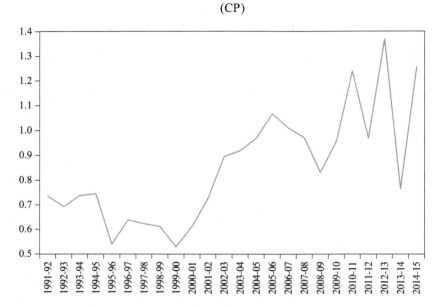

Figure 4.9(a) Capital Productivity (Level)

DIFCP

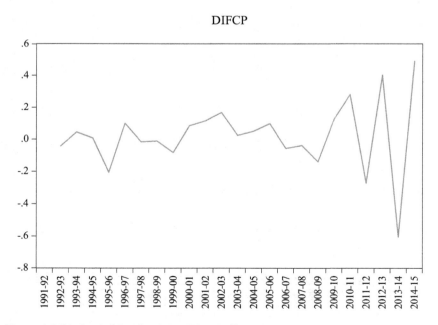

Figure 4.9(b) Capital Productivity (First Difference)

(ULC)

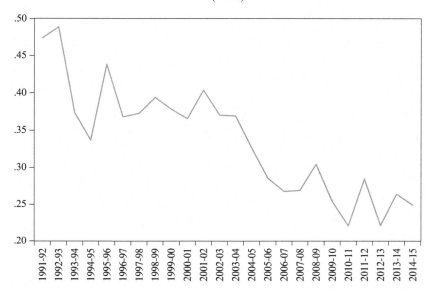

Figure 4.10(a) Unit Labour Cost (Level)

DIFULC

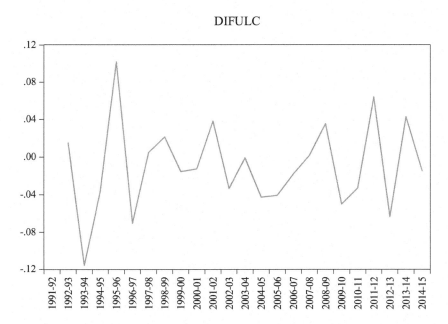

Figure 4.10(b) Unit Labour Cost (First Difference)

(ER)

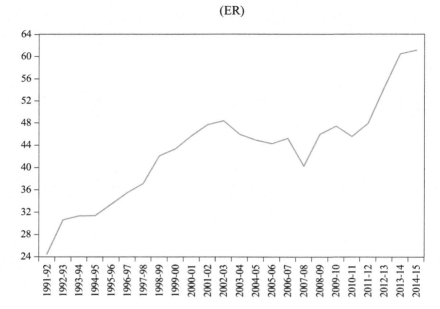

Figure 4.11(a) Exchange Rate (Level)

DIFER

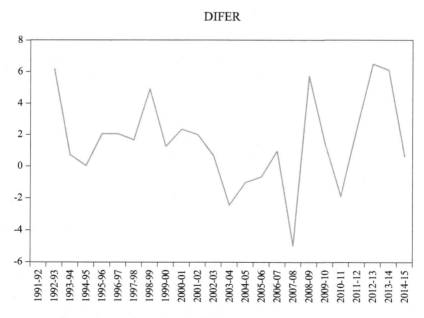

Figure 4.11(b) Exchange Rate (First Difference)

(REER)

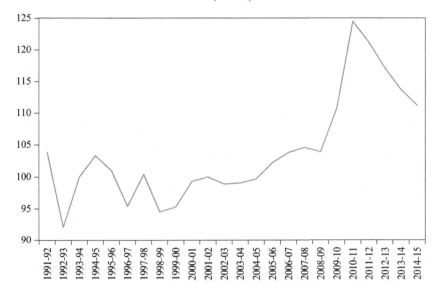

Figure 4.12(a) Real Effective Exchange Rate (Level)

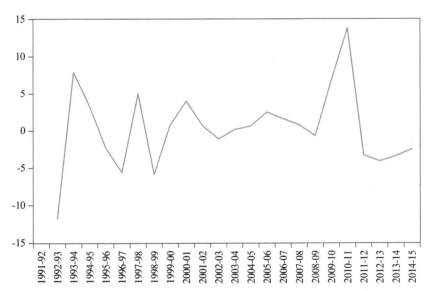

Figure 4.12(b) Real Effective Exchange Rate (First Difference)

Source: On the basis of data compiled and generated on EViews software by author.

Optimal lag length selection

In the present study, the values of AIC and SC are minimum, i.e. 4.022 and 7.890, respectively, for lag length two. Hence we go with selecting two lags for the further analysis.

Granger causality test

The findings of this test are given in Table 4.14 and show the presence of feedback effects (bi-directional) and uni-directional effects. The results show the presence of bi-directional effects in case of ULC and only uni-directional causality running from LP and ER to EC, which indicates that the selected variables have effects on the EC of the 'Textiles' group. However, no causality is found running from CP and REER to EC. These findings support the study conducted by Kordalska and Olczyk (2014); Ito and Shimizu (2015).

Johansen and Juselius co-integration test

Tables 4.15 and 4.16 highlight the findings of trace and maximum Eigen value statistics from which the number of co-integrated equations or long relationship

Table 4.14 Granger Causality Test ('Textiles' Group)

Null Hypothesis	F-Statistic	Prob*.	Results	Direction
LP does not Granger Cause EC	1.854	0.031	C	Uni-directional
EC does not Granger Cause LP	0.199	0.821	NC	
CP does not Granger Cause EC	1.071	0.365	NC	None
EC does not Granger Cause CP	1.008	0.386	NC	
ULC does not Granger Cause EC	3.610	0.049	C	Bi-directional
EC does not Granger Cause ULC	3.218	0.047	C	
ER does not Granger Cause EC	1.479	0.023	C	Uni-directional
EC does not Granger Cause ER	0.064	0.938	NC	
REER does not Granger Cause EC	0.069	0.9333	NC	None
EC does not Granger Cause REER	1.375	0.2811	NC	

Source: Author's own calculations.

* Significant at 5 percent level.
C stands for 'Causality' and NC for 'No Causality.'

between the variables can be examined for the 'Textiles' group. The null hypothesis is rejected when estimated value of trace statistics and maximum Eigen value statistics is more than the critical values at 5 percent significance level. The findings of the test reveal that both the trace test and maximum Eigen value statistics have five co-integrated equations in the model, which reveals the long-run relationship between the select variables for the 'Textiles' group.

From the Table 4.17, it is clear that the values of R-squared and adjusted R-squared in the model are 0.848 and 0.806, respectively. This indicates that all the variables such as LP, CP, ULC, ER, and REER have a significant influence on the EC of the 'Textiles' group. The results of the study also support the findings of Chan, Au, and Sarkar (2008).

Table 4.15 Johansen and Juselius Co-integration Test: Trace Statistics

Testing the Existence and No. of Co-integration Relationships

Hypothesis (No. of Co-integration Equations)	Trace Statistics	0.05 Critical Value	Prob.
None	233.664	95.753	0.000
At most 1	151.005	69.818	0.000
At most 2	88.539	47.856	0.000
At most 3	51.897	29.797	0.000
At most 4	20.622	15.494	0.007
At most 5	0.282	3.841	0.595

Source: Author's own calculations.

Table 4.16 Johansen and Juselius Co-integration Test: Max Eigen Statistics

Testing the Existence and No. of Co-integration Relationships

Null Hypothesis	Max Eigen value	0.05 Critical Value	Prob.
None	82.659	40.077	0.000
At most 1	62.465	33.876	0.000
At most 2	36.641	27.584	0.002
At most 3	31.274	21.131	0.001
At most 4	20.340	14.264	0.004
At most 5	0.282	3.841	0.595

Source: Author's own calculations.

Table 4.17 Regression Results

R-squared	Adjusted R-squared	F-statistic	Prob. (F-statistic)
0.848	0.806	20.233	0.000

Source: Author's own calculations.

Table 4.18 Result of the Error Correction Model

Variable	Coefficient	Probability
C(1)	−0.8382	0.0484
C(2)	−2.6051	0.5599
C(3)	−15.8178	0.0753
C(4)	−5.9057	0.8580
C(5)	0.0154	0.9473
C(6)	−0.2581	0.2635
C(7)	5.9574	0.2187
C(8)	3.5961	0.7160
C(9)	34.8847	0.1296
C(10)	0.0591	0.7659
C(11)	0.0213	0.9026
C(12)	0.3801	0.4691

Source: Author's own calculations.

R-squared = 0.930.

Results of vector error correction model

The results of the VECM are presented in Table 4.18 and reveal that the long-run coefficient of co-integrating model C(1) is negative and significant. Hence, it can be concluded that there is long-run causality running from IVs, i.e. LP, CP, ULC, ER, and REER, to the DV, i.e. EC for the 'Textiles' group. The ECM model for this case is given by

D(EC,2) = C(1)*(D (EC(−1))−0.5173* D (REER(−1)) −0.1311) + C(2)*D (LP(−1)) 0.0114* D(REER(−1))−0.1506) + C(3)* (D(CP (−1)) + 0.0175*D (REER(−1))−0.0215) + C(4)*(D (ULC(−1)) + 0.0006* D(REER(−1)) + 0.0100) + C(5)*(D (ER(−1)) + 1.1100*D (REER(−1)) −2.5636) + C(6)* D(EC(−1),2) +C(7)*D(LP(−1),2) + C(8)* D(CP(−1),2) + C(9)*D(ULC(−1),2) + C(10)* D(ER(−1),2) + C(11)* D(REER(−1),2) + C(12)

where C(1) is the coefficient of co-integrating model or error correction term in long-run, C(12) is constant and C(2) to C(11) are short-run coefficients.

After estimating the long-run causality from IVs to DV, now the short-run causality running from IVs to DV has been estimated using the Wald test. Table 4.19 presents Chi-square test statistics to test the null hypothesis that the cause variable does not affect the effect variable along with the *p*-values. From the table, it can be inferred that Chi-square test statistics is significant at 5 percent level of significance for CP and ULC. Hence the null hypothesis can be rejected; there is no short-run causality running from IVs to DV. Hence, there is short-run causality running from CP and ULC to EC (Dhiman, Forthcoming). These findings also support Ito and Shimizu (2015).

Table 4.19 Short-Run Causality (Wald Test)

Variables	Probability
LP	0.2336
CP	0.0271*
ULC	0.0121*
ER	0.9113
REER	0.8998

Source: Author's own calculations.

Note: *indicates significant at 5 percent level of significance.

Table 4.20 Diagnostic Test

Test	Null Hypotheses	Value
Normality Test (Jarque–Bera Statistic)	Null Hypotheses: Residuals are normally distributed	0.617 (0.621)
Serial Correlation (Breusch-Godfrey Serial Correlation LM Test)	Null Hypotheses: Residuals are not serially correlated	0.723 (0.306)
Heteroskedasticity Test (Breusch-Pagan-Godfrey)	Null Hypotheses: Residuals are not heteroskedastic	1.764 (0.413)

Source: Author's own calculations.

Note: Values in parentheses "()" indicate the *p*-value.

However for LP, ER, and REER, there is no short-run causality running from LP, ER, and REER to EC, as *p*-values are non-significant at the 5 percent level of significance. This finding is also supported by Gotur (1985) and Koray and Lastrapes (1989).

So the summary of the model is that there is long-run causality running from IVs, i.e. LP, CP, ULC, ER, and REER to the DV and short-run causality running from CP and ULC to EC. The null hypothesis of the Wald test is given by

$$C(2) = C(7) = 0; \ C(3) = C(8) = 0; \ C(4) = C(9) = 0; \ C(5) = C(10) = 0; \ C(11) = 0$$

Diagnostic test

The regression result indicated high *R*-squared value (0.930), which is high, so the model can be accepted and can proceed with further diagnostic tests. Table 4.20 displays the results of the diagnostic test for the VECM, which suggest that the model is normally distributed with a probability of Jarque–Bera statistics more than 5 percent. The model also does not suffer from the problems of serial correlation and heteroskedasticity. The probability values of *F*-statistic of Breusch-Godfrey serial correlation LM test and Breusch-Pagan-Godfrey test are more than 5 percent. These values reveal that the model has the property of goodness of fit.

The 'Textile Products' group

The share of India's 'Textile Products' group exports in its total output, the growth behaviour of select determinants, and empirical results are discussed as follows:

Share of 'Textile Products' exports in total output

Table 4.21 shows the ratio of textile exports to the total output of the Indian 'Textile Products' group. It is seen that this ratio increased from

Table 4.21 Share of Textile Exports in Total Output of Indian 'Textile Products' Group

Year	Total Output (in Rs. Crore)	Textile Exports (in Rs. Crore)	Ratio of Textile Exports to Total Output (in %)
1991–92	5343	2617	39.98
1992–93	6425	2803	54.15
1993–94	9595	3300	38.58
1994–95	12105	3617	35.69
1995–96	15087	4167	35.83
1996–97	14926	4552	42.31
1997–98	17764	4931	38.99
1998–99	20583	5848	42.06
1999–00	26947	6437	40.37
2000–01	30448	6591	42.21
2001–02	25898	5957	53.34
2002–03	32920	7640	50.17
2003–04	35167	6459	53.30
2004–05	45842	6271	44.05
2005–06	54100	7722	45.06
2006–07	81017	8020	46.67
2007–08	65678	7808	48.86
2008–09	89567	7006	47.46
2009–10	99333	7595	50.31
2010–11	115453	10282	53.34
2011–12	125645	11036	54.72
2012–13	136423	13,854	55.63
2013–14	180372	14,136	57.22
2014–15	165753	14,798	58.61

Source: The author.

39.98 percent in 1991–92 and reached 53.34 percent in 2003–04. Thereafter, a declining trend can be observed till 2008–09, and the share was 47.46 percent. Thereafter, increasing trend can be observed, and the share of textile exports in total output of the Indian 'Textile Products' group was 58.61 percent in 2014–15.

Growth behaviour of export competitiveness and its determinants

Table 4.22 reveals the growth behaviour of determinants of EC of the Indian 'Textile Products' group. The table shows that the ratio of exports of the Indian 'Textile Products' group to its output increased from 39.98 percent in 1991–92 and attained its maximum level of 58.61 percent in 2014–15 (with some fluctuations).

Regarding the factors affecting competitiveness, the table also shows that the value of labour productivity increased from Rs. 0.70 lakh in 1991–92 to the

Table 4.22 Growth Behaviour of Export Competitiveness of 'Textile Products' Group and Its Determinants

Years	Export Competitiveness	Labour Productivity (in Rs. Lakh)	Capital Productivity (in Rs.)	Unit Labour Cost (in Rs. Lakh)	Exchange Rate (in Dollars)	Real Effective Exchange Rate
1991–92	39.98	0.70	1.81	0.20	24.47	103.84
1992–93	54.15	0.70	1.87	0.22	30.64	92.1
1993–94	38.58	0.99	2.05	0.16	31.36	100
1994–95	35.69	1.03	1.66	0.18	31.39	103.3
1995–96	35.83	1.04	1.44	0.20	33.44	101
1996–97	42.31	1.03	1.56	0.22	35.49	95.41
1997–98	38.99	0.97	1.37	0.26	37.16	100.4
1998–99	42.06	1.17	1.79	0.25	42.07	94.52
1999–00	40.37	1.33	1.42	0.22	43.33	95.29
2000–01	42.21	1.27	1.51	0.25	45.68	99.3
2001–02	53.34	1.17	1.77	0.28	47.69	100
2002–03	50.17	1.28	2.04	0.28	48.39	98.9
2003–04	53.30	1.15	1.97	0.31	45.95	99.04
2004–05	44.05	1.25	2.04	0.31	44.93	99.68
2005–06	45.06	1.27	2.27	0.32	44.27	102.2
2006–07	46.67	1.21	1.59	0.29	45.24	103.8
2007–08	48.86	1.51	2.30	0.31	40.26	104.6
2008–09	47.46	1.68	2.05	0.31	45.99	103.9
2009–10	50.31	1.73	2.11	0.32	47.44	110.7
2010–11	53.34	1.97	2.11	0.34	45.56	124.5
2011–12	54.72	2.08	2.18	0.34	47.92	121.2
2012–13	55.63	2.42	2.03	0.34	54.4	117.1
2013–14	57.22	2.78	2.81	0.32	60.5	113.7
2014–15	58.61	2.87	2.76	0.30	61.14	111.2

Source: The author.

maximum level of Rs. 2.87 lakh in 2014–15. Capital productivity decreased from Rs. 1.81 in 1991–92 to Rs. 1.37 in 1997–98. After this period, fluctuations can be seen in the capital productivity, and it was Rs.2.76 in 2014–15. ULC decreased from Rs. 0.20 lakh in 1991–92 to Rs. 0.16 lakh in 1993–94. Thereafter, an increasing trend can be observed, and labour cost attained the maximum level of Rs. 0.34 lakh in 2010–11, which remained stagnant till 2012–13. The recorded value of ULC in 2014–15 was Rs. 0.30 lakh. The ER of the rupee in terms of dollars increased from Rs. 24.47 in 1991–92 to Rs. 61.14 in 2014–15, indicating depreciation of the Indian rupee against the dollar. REER has been continuously depreciating with some fluctuations.

Empirical results

The empirical results of various techniques of analysis are presented in this section for the Indian 'Textile Products' group.

ADF test

Table 4.23 shows the results of the ADF test for all the variables used in the analysis at levels as well as at first difference. The number of lags used in the test is determined by a Schwartz Bayesian information criterion. From the results exhibited in Table 4.23, it can be seen that, at levels, all the variables are non-stationary, and they are stationary at first difference. The graphs of stationarity (see Figures 4.13 to 4.18) are also presented for each variable at the level and the first difference for the 'Textile Products' group.

Optimal lag length selection

In the present study, the values of AIC and SC are minimum, i.e. 9.032 and 11.403, respectively, for lag length two. Hence two lags are selected for the purpose of further analysis.

Granger causality test

The findings of this test are given in Table 4.24 and show the presence of uni-directional effects and no effects. The results show the presence of only uni-directional causality running from LP, CP, ULC, and ER to EC, which indicates that the selected variables have effects on the EC of the 'Textile Products' group. However, no causality is found running from REER to EC. These findings support the work of Jian (2007).

Johansen and Juselius co-integration test

Tables 4.25 and 4.26 highlight the findings of trace and maximum Eigen value statistics from which the number of co-integrated equations or long

Table 4.23 Augmented Dickey-Fuller (ADF) Unit Root Test of the Variables for Textile Products

Variables	At level				At first difference			
	t-Statistic	Critical values at 5%	Prob.*	Result	t-Statistic	Critical values at 5%	Prob.*	Result
Export Competitiveness	-1.941	-2.998	0.308	Non-stationary	-7.532	-3.004	0.000	Stationary
Labour Productivity	1.651	-2.998	0.999	Non-stationary	-3.912	-3.004	0.007	Stationary
Capital Productivity	-1.720	-2.998	0.408	Non-stationary	-7.897	-3.004	0.000	Stationary
Unit Labour Cost	-1.460	-2.998	0.535	Non-stationary	-5.025	-3.004	0.000	Stationary
Exchange Rate	-0.917	-2.998	0.764	Non-stationary	-4.427	-3.004	0.002	Stationary
Real Effective Exchange rate	-1.372	-2.998	0.577	Non-stationary	-5.478	-3.004	0.000	Stationary

Source: The author.

EC

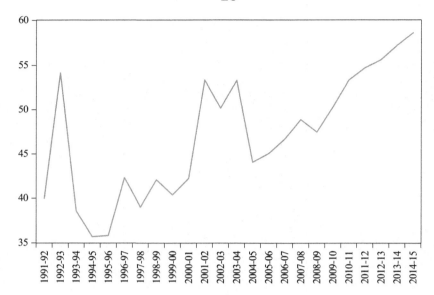

Figure 4.13(a) Export Competitiveness (Level) (Textile Industry)

DIFEC

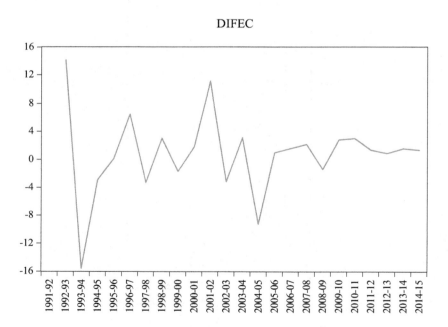

Figure 4.13(b) Export Competitiveness (First Difference)

(LP)

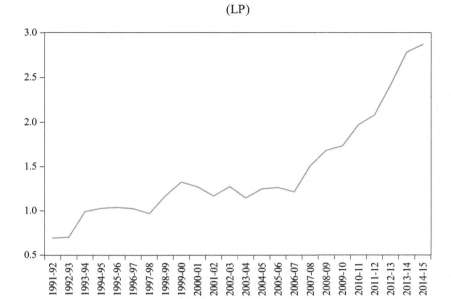

Figure 4.14(a) Labour Productivity (Level)

DIFLP

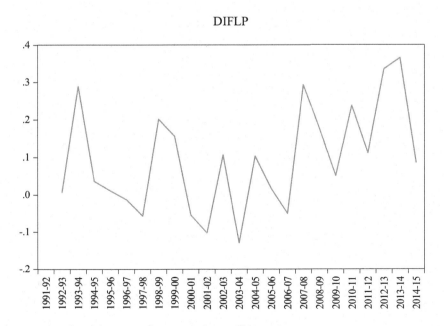

Figure 4.14(b) Labour Productivity (First Difference)

(CP)

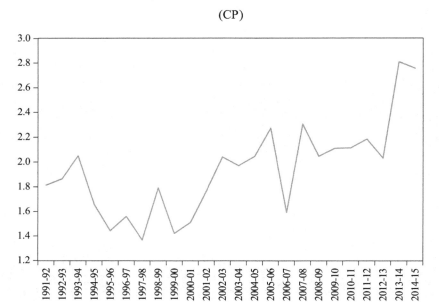

Figure 4.15(a) Capital Productivity (Level)

DIFCP

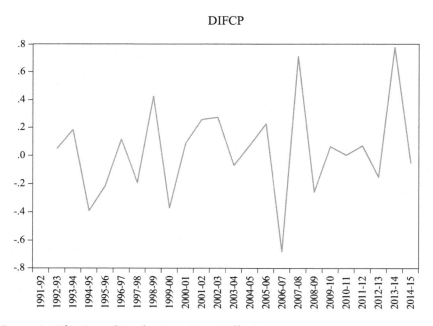

Figure 4.15(b) Capital Productivity (First Difference)

(ULC)

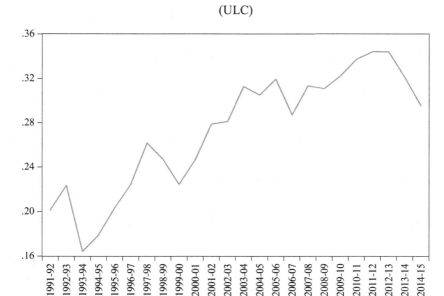

Figure 4.16(a) Unit Labour Cost (Level)

DIFULC

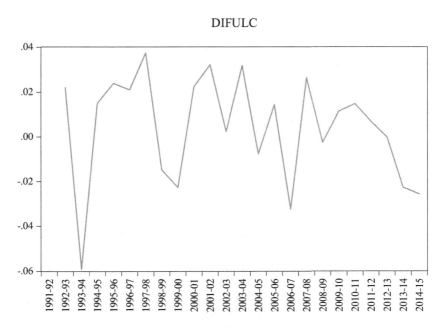

Figure 4.16(b) Unit Labour Cost (First Difference)

(ER)

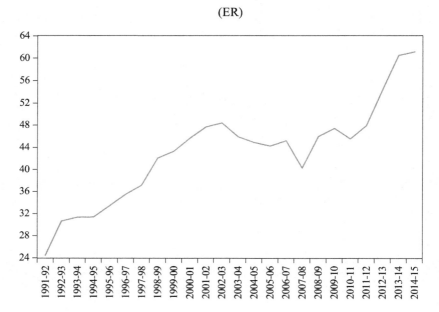

Figure 4.17(a) Exchange Rate (Level)

DIFER

Figure 4.17(b) Exchange Rate (First Difference)

(REER)

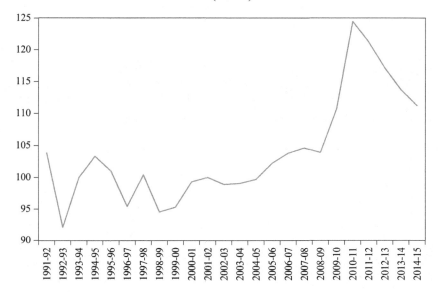

Figure 4.18(a) Real Effective Exchange Rate (Level)

DIFREER

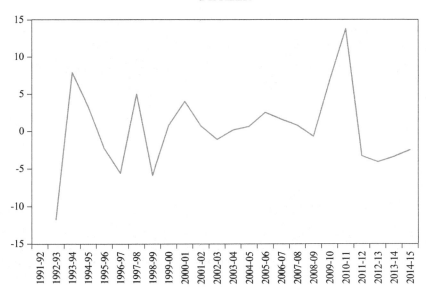

Figure 4.18(b) Real Effective Exchange Rate (First Difference)

Source: On the basis of data compiled and generated on EViews software by author.

Table 4.24 Granger Causality Test ('Textile Products' Group)

Null Hypothesis	F-Statistic	Prob*.	Results	Direction
LP does not Granger Cause EC	2.631	0.015	C	Uni-directional
EC does not Granger Cause LP	0.738	0.493	NC	
CP does not Granger Cause EC	3.846	0.043	C	Uni-directional
EC does not Granger Cause CP	1.381	0.279	NC	
ULC does not Granger Cause EC	1.214	0.031	C	Uni-directional
EC does not Granger Cause ULC	0.452	0.643	NC	
ER does not Granger Cause EC	2.651	0.038	C	Uni-directional
EC does not Granger Cause ER	0.043	0.957	NC	
REER does not Granger Cause EC	0.282	0.757	NC	None
EC does not Granger Cause REER	0.207	0.814	NC	

Source: Author's own calculations.

* Significant at 5 percent level; C stands for 'Causality' and NC for 'No Causality.'

Table 4.25 Johansen and Juselius Co-integration Test: Trace Statistics

Testing the Existence and No. of Co-integration Relationships

Hypothesis (No. of Co-integration Equations)	Trace Statistics	0.05 Critical Value	Prob.
None	125.955	95.753	0.000
At most 1	82.013	69.818	0.003
At most 2	48.622	47.856	0.042
At most 3	27.191	29.797	0.097
At most 4	10.762	15.494	0.226
At most 5	0.443	3.841	0.505

Source: Author's own calculations.

relationship between the variable can be examined for the 'Textile Products' group. The findings of the test reveal that the trace test has three co-integrating equations and maximum Eigen value statistics have one co-integrated equation in the model which reveals the long-run relationship between the select variables for the 'Textile Products' group.

From Table 4.27, it is clear that the values of R-squared and adjusted R-squared in the model are 0.694 and 0.609, respectively. This indicates

Table 4.26 Johansen and Juselius Co-integration Test: Max Eigen Statistics

Testing the Existence and No. of Co-integration Relationships

Hypothesis (No. of Co-integration Equations)	Max Eigen value	0.05 Critical Value	Prob.
None	43.9415	40.0775	0.0175
At most 1	33.3911	33.8768	0.0570
At most 2	21.4309	27.5843	0.2510
At most 3	16.4286	21.1316	0.2008
At most 4	10.3194	14.2646	0.1918
At most 5	0.4433	3.8414	0.5055

Source: Author's own calculations.

Table 4.27 Regression Results

R-squared	Adjusted R-squared	F-statistic	Prob. (F-statistic)
0.6945	0.6096	89.1855	0.0003

Source: Author's own calculations.

that all the variables such as LP, CP, ULC, ER, and REER have significant influence on the EC of the 'Textile Products' group. This impact of IVs on DVs is lower as compared to that of the textile industry and the 'Textiles' group. These findings support the studies of Cheung and Sengupta (2013); Kathuria (2013).

Results of vector error correction model

The results of the VECM are presented in Table 4.28 and reveal that the long-run coefficient of co-integrating model C(1) is negative and significant. Hence, it can be concluded that there is long-run causality running from independent IVs, i.e. LP, CP, ULC, ER, and REER, to the DV, i.e. EC for the 'Textile Products' group. The ECM model generated is as follows:

$$D(EC,2) = C(1)*(D(EC(-1)) + 91.6249*D(ULC(-1)) + 0.2058*D(ER(-1))$$
$$0.2166*D(REER(-1)) - 0.6429) + C(2)*(D(LP(-1)) + 5.7901*D(ULC(-1))$$
$$-0.0319*D(ER(-1))\ 0.0421*D(REER(-1))\ -0.037) + C(3)*(D(CP(-1))$$
$$+\ 7.4559*D(ULC(-1))\ +0.0233*D(ER(-1))\ +\ 0.0006*D(REER(-1))$$
$$-0.1135) + C(4)*D(EC(-1),2) + C(5)*D(LP(-1),2) + C(6)*D(CP(-1),2)$$
$$+ C(7)*D(ULC(-1),2) + C(8)*D(ER(-1),2) + C(9)*D(REER(-1),2) + C(10)$$

where C(1) is the coefficient of co-integrating model or error correction term in long-run, C(10) is constant and C(2) to C(9) are short-run coefficients.

Table 4.28 Result of the Error Correction Model

Variable	Coefficient	Probability
C(1)	–0.533	0.050
C(2)	–7.838	0.295
C(3)	–7.795	0.199
C(4)	–0.390	0.075
C(5)	0.255	0.975
C(6)	7.596	0.069
C(7)	115.072	0.015
C(8)	1.189	0.005
C(9)	0.037	0.863
C(10)	0.540	0.528

Source: Author's own calculations.

R-squared = 0.8478.

Table 4.29 Short-Run Causality (Wald Test)

Variables	Probability
LP	0.442
CP	0.108
ULC	0.004*
ER	0.000*
REER	0.860

Source: Author's own calculations.

Note: * indicates significant at 5 percent level of significance.

After estimating the long-run causality from IVs to DV, now the short-run causality running from IVs to DV is examined using Wald test. Table 4.29 presents Chi-square test statistics to test the null hypothesis that the cause variable does not affect the effect variable along with the p-values. From the table, it can be inferred that Chi-square test statistics are significant at 5 percent level of significance for ULC and ER. So the null hypothesis that there is no short-run causality running from IVs to DV can be rejected. Hence, there is short-run causality running from ULC and ER to EC. These findings are in line with Chan et al. (2008); Jaussaud and Rey (2012). However for LP, CP, and REER, there is no short-run causality running from LP, CP, and REER to EC, as p-values are non-significant at a 5 percent level of significance.

The summary of the model is that long-run causality running from IVs, i.e. LP, CP, ULC, ER, and REER, to the DV, i.e. EC and there is short-run causality running from ULC and ER to EC.

Table 4.30 Diagnostic Test

Test	Null Hypotheses	Value
Normality Test (Jarque–Bera Statistic)	Null Hypotheses: Residuals are normally distributed	1.352 (0.508)
Serial Correlation (Breusch-Godfrey Serial Correlation LM Test)	Null Hypotheses: Residuals are not serially correlated	1.835 (0.076)
Heteroskedasticity Test (Breusch-Pagan-Godfrey)	Null Hypotheses: Residuals are not heteroskedastic	0.171 (0.981)

Source: Author's own calculations.

Note: Values in parentheses " ()"indicate the *p*-value.

The null hypothesis of the Wald test is:

$$C(2) = C(5) = 0; C(3) = C(6) = 0; C(7) = 0; C(8) = 0; C(9) = 0$$

Diagnostic test

The regression result indicated high *R*-squared value (0.8478), which is high, so the model can be accepted, and further diagnostic tests can be performed. Table 4.30 displays the results of the diagnostic test for the VECM, which suggest that the model is normally distributed with a probability of Jarque–Bera statistics more than 5 percent. The model also does not suffer from the problems of serial correlation and heteroskedasticity. The probability values of *F*-statistic of Breusch-Godfrey serial correlation LM test and Breusch-Pagan-Godfrey test are more than 5 percent. These values reveal that the model has the property of goodness of fit.

Concluding remarks

From the results and discussion of the textile industry and its two groups, the 'Textiles' group and the 'Textile Products' group, it can be concluded that the select determinants have different relationships with the EC for the textile industry and its two groups. The findings of the Granger causality test show the presence of only uni-directional causality and absence of feedback effects in case of the textile industry. However, feedback effects or bi-directional relationship of ULC with EC is found in case of the 'Textiles' group and only uni-directional causality running from LP and ER to EC. In case of the 'Textile Products' group, the findings of the Granger causality test show the presence of only uni-directional causality running from LP, CP, ULC, and ER to EC. The findings of the Johansen and Juselius co-integration test reveal the long-run relationship between the select variables for the Indian textile industry and its two groups, the 'Textiles' group and the 'Textile Products' group. The regression model also highlights that the values of R-squared and adjusted R-squared are high for the textile industry and its two groups. The results of the VECM to examine the long-run coefficient of the co-integrating model reveals that there is no long-run causality running from IVs, i.e. LP, CP, ULC, ER, and REER, to the DV, i.e. EC in case of the textile industry. However, there is the presence of long-run causality running from independent variables (IVs) to DV in case of the 'Textiles' group and the 'Textile Products' group. The results of the diagnostic test for the VECM suggest that the model is normally distributed, and the model also does not suffer from the problems of serial correlation and heteroskedasticity. So it can be concluded that all the models have the property of goodness of fit for the textile industry and its two groups.

References

Abraham, V., and Sasikumar, S. K. (2011). Labor cost and export behavior of firms in Indian textile and clothing industry. *Economics, Management and Financial Markets*, 6(1), 258–282.

Aung, N. G. (2009). *Time series data analysis using EViews*. Hoboken, NJ: John Wiley & Sons.

Balassa, B. (1978). Exports and economic growth: Further evidence. *Journal of Development Economics*, 5(2), 181–189.

Banik, N. (2008). India's exports: An analysis. *ASCI Journal of Management*, 37(2), 151–163.

Bhattacharya, B., and Mukherjee, J. (2008). *Indian equity market since liberalization: Efficiency, volatility and structural break*. Kolkata: World View Publishers.

Bhattacharya, B., and Mukherjee, J. (2016). Foreign direct investment and macroeconomic indicators in India: A causality analysis. In M. Roy and S. S. Roy (Eds.), *International trade and international finance: Explorations of contemporary issues* (pp.363–371). New Delhi: Springer.

Broll, U., and Eckwert, B. (1999). Exchange rate volatility and international trade. *Southern Economic Journal*, 66, 178–185.

Chan, E. M. H., Au, K. F., and Sarkar, M. K. (2008). Antecedents to India's textile exports: 1985–2005. *International Journal of Indian Culture and Business Management*, 1(3), 265–276.

Cheung, Y. W., and Sengupta, S. (2013). Impact of exchange rate movements on exports: An analysis of Indian non-financial sector firms. *Journal of International Money and Finance*, 39, 231–245.

De Grauwe, P., and Verfaille, G. (1988). Exchange rate variability, misalignment, and the European monetary system. In *Misalignment of exchange rates: Effects on trade and industry* (pp.77–104). Chicago: University of Chicago Press.

Dhiman, R. (Forthcoming). Cointegration and causality testing for capital productivity, labour cost and export competitiveness of Indian textile industry. *International Journal of Business and Globalisation*.

Dickey, D. A., and Fuller, W. A. (1979). Distribution of the estimators for autoregressive time series with a unit root. *Journal of the American Statistical Association*, 74(366a), 427–431.

Engle, R. F., and Granger, C. W. (1987). Co-integration and error correction: Representation, estimation, and testing. *Econometrica: Journal of the Econometric Society*, 55(2), 251–276.

Fang, W., Lai, Y., and Miller, S. (2004). *Export promotion through exchange rate policy: Exchange rate depreciation or stabilization?* Department of Economics, University of Connecticut, Working Papers, 2005–2007.

Fayissa, B. (1996). Capital, research & development, trade, and economic growth. *Economia Internazionale/International Economics*, 49(3), 373–384.

Gotur, P. (1985). Effects of exchange rate volatility on trade: Some further evidence. *Staff Papers*, 32(3), 475–512.

Grossman, G., and Helpman, E. (1991). *Innovation and growth in the global economy*. Cambridge: MIT Press.

Gujarati, D. N., and Porter, D. C. (2009). *Basic econometrics*. Boston: McGraw-Hill.

Hong, K. (1997). Foreign capital and economic growth in Korea: 1970–1990. *Journal of Economic Development*, 22(1), 79–89.

Ito, K., and Shimizu, J. (2015). Industry-level competitiveness, productivity and effective exchange rates in East Asia. *Asian Economic Journal*, 29(2), 181–214.

Jaussaud, J., and Rey, S. (2012). Long-run determinants Japanese export to China and the United States: A sectoral analysis. *Pacific Economic Review*, 17(1), 1–28.

Jian, L. Ü. (2007). Empirical study on the influence of RMB exchange rate misalignment on China's export. *Frontiers of Economics in China*, 2(2), 224–236.

Johansen, S. (1988). Statistical analysis of cointegration vectors. *Journal of Economic Dynamics and Control*, 12(2–3), 231–254.

Johansen, S., and Juselius, K. (1990). Maximum likelihood estimation and inference on cointegration—with applications to the demand for money. *Oxford Bulletin of Economics and Statistics*, 52(2), 169–210.

Kathuria, M. L. (2013). Analyzing competitiveness of clothing export sector of India and Bangladesh: Dynamic revealed comparative advantage approach. *Competitiveness Review: An International Business Journal*, 23(2), 131–157.

Khatun, R. (2016). Relation between trade in financial services and economic growth in BRICS economies: Co-integration and causality approach. *Global Business Review*, 17(1), 214–225.

Koray, F., and Lastrapes, W. D. (1989). Real exchange rate volatility and US bilateral trade: A VAR approach. *Review of Economics and Statistics*, 71(4), 708–712.

Kordalska, A., and Olczyk, M. (2014). Impact of the manufacturing sector on the export competitiveness of European countries–a spatial panel analysis. *Comparative Economic Research*, 17(4), 105–121.

Kumar, N., and Siddharthan, N. S. (1994). Technology, firm size and export behavior in developing countries: The case of Indian enterprises. *The Journal of Development Studies*, 31(2), 289–309.

Prakash, V. J., Nauriyal, K. D., and Kaur, S. (2017). Assessing financial integration of BRICS equity markets: An empirical analysis. *Emerging Economy Studies*, 3(2), 1–12.

Rivera-Batiz, L. A., and Romer, P. (1991). Economic integration and endogenous growth. *The Quarterly Journal of Economics*, 106(2), 531–555.

Tsang, W. Y., and Au, K. F. (2008). Textile and clothing exports of selected South and Southeast Asian countries. *Journal of Fashion Marketing and Management: An International Journal*, 12(4), 565–578.

Wubneh, M. (1990). State control and manufacturing labor productivity in Ethiopia. *The Journal of Developing Areas*, 24(3), 311–326.

5 Summing up and policy implications

Introduction

The Indian textile industry stands out in the world economy, and it also has extraordinary importance for the developing economies. The Indian textile industry has been well known for its textile products for a very long time. This is primarily due to cheap labour. The Indian textile industry has played an essential role through its contribution to industrial output, gaining foreign exchange reserves, and employment generation.

After the economic reforms of 1991, the industry witnessed liberalization of trade, and the boundaries for trade are not restricted now. This turned out to be a stimulus for the textile industry. The economic reforms were supplemented with the removal of the quota regime from January 1, 2005, as per the World Trade Organisation (WTO) Agreement on Textile and Clothing (ATC). The elimination of the quotas has shaped new prospects for developing nations but has also exposed them to added competition as a threat. The economic reforms have brought new opportunities for the Indian textile industry, but at the same time, the reforms have also imposed certain challenges, particularly from cheaper imports. In addition to this, export competitiveness (EC) is another challenge that needs to be addressed to sustain position in the international market. Hence, it can be concluded that the textile industry has to battle for its share in the global textile trade. There is no doubt that the economic reforms have relaxed the barriers to the trade, but this in no way will guarantee growth in the export shares, and only the fittest will survive. The major findings of the book and policy implications are discussed in this chapter.

The growth of the Indian textile industry and its two groups

Textile exports of India increased significantly from US$4865.3 million in 1991 to US$37162 million in 2015, with a compound annual growth rate (CAGR) of 9.2 percent. The CAGR of textile exports from 1991–2002 was 7.85 percent, and it improved in 2003–2015 to 10.22 percent.

India's share in the total world exports of textile and clothing had historically been small, but it began to grow significantly after 1991, reaching 2.68 percent of world exports in 1998 and 4.99 percent in 2015. The good part is that India's share in world textile exports increased in 2007 and 2008 despite the slow-down in the economies of some of the major importing countries such as the U.S. and increased competition from our neighbouring countries like China, Bangladesh, etc. The industry's share in world exports of textiles and apparel is still quite low as compared to other nations, including the Asian giants like China, South Korea, Singapore, and Hong Kong. So it can be concluded that India's share in world textile exports has improved from 2.02 percent in 1991 to 4.9 percent in 2015, but still this cannot be regarded as a significant improvement due to the fact that the industry has a strength of cheap labour as compared to the rest of the countries. However, the percentage contribution of textile exports in total exports has declined continuously from 25.5 percent in 1991 to 14.05 percent in 2015. This can be attributed to the fact that commodities other than textiles have also shown remarkable growth in the world market, particularly gems and jewellery, transport equipment, and electronic goods.

After observing the growth rates of the Indian textile industry and its two groups, 'Textiles' and 'Textile Products,' it becomes clear that the performance of the group 'Textile Products' was better in respect of the number of factories, gross value added, number of employees, and capital stock. This could, to a certain extent, be attributed to the fact that the clothing sector was de-reserved from the small-scale industry sector in the year 2000. So it can be concluded that the 'Textile Products' group was better prepared for the free trade regime than the 'Textiles' group during the study period. Consequently, employment in the textile industry could well turn out to be much more dependent on the 'Textile Products' group as compared to the 'Textiles' group in the time to come.

Trends in labour and capital productivity

There was a marginal increase in growth rate of labour productivity (LP) in the 'Textiles' group during the study period, while the growth rate of labour productivity in the 'Textile Products' group was comparatively lower during this period. The labour productivity in the Indian textile industry grew at a slower rate in comparison to the 'Textiles' group. The LP in case of the 'Textile Products' group was lowest during the study period. Capital productivity (CP) in the 'Textiles' group declined marginally as compared to the textile industry, while the growth rate of CP in the 'Textile Products' group was lowest during the study period. On the whole, the CP in the Indian textile industry increased during this period in comparison to the 'Textiles' and 'Textile Products' group.

So we can conclude that the CP came out as an issue of concern for the entire textile industry and its two groups. For the 'Textile' and the 'Textile Products' groups, the CP in sub-period-I is very low and has not improved significantly for the entire period. Thus, appropriate strategies need to be developed to ensure the easier and cheaper availability of capital imports to the textile firms. A number of previous studies such as Bedi and Cororaton (2008) and USITC (2001) also highlighted the low level of technology in case of the Indian textile industry.

Export performance of Indian textile exports

The product-wise analysis of the performance of India's textile exports at the HS two-digit level reveals that total textile exports increased at a compound annual growth rate of 7.85 percent during sub-period-I, 10.22 percent during sub-period-II, and 9.2 percent during the whole period. It must be noted that the lowest growth rate of 0.68 percent was recorded in case of 'Carpets and other textile floor coverings' (HS Code 57) in both sub-periods-I and II. 'Wadding, felt, nonwovens, yarns, twine, cordage, etc' (HS 56) has shown rapid growth during both the sub-periods, which indicate better prospects for the future. 'Silk' (HS 50) showed a significant increase during sub-period-I, but its performance declined in the second sub-period. The commodities which significantly performed better in sub-period-II are 'Wool, animal hair, horsehair yarn and fabric' (HS 51), 'Cotton' (HS 52), 'Vegetable textile fibres, paper yarn, woven fabric' (HS 53), 'Manmade filaments' (HS 54), 'Carpets and other textile floor coverings' (HS 57), 'Impregnated, coated or laminated textile fabric' (HS 59), and 'Knitted or crocheted fabric' (HS 60). However, the growth performance of 'Special woven or tufted fabric, lace, tapestry etc.' declined in sub-period-II. The product-wise analysis of the performance of India's textile exports at the HS four-digit level is presented in what follows.

Silk (HS 50) product group

During the study period, four products experienced growth rates higher than the growth rate of the group (2.15 percent). The highest growth rate of 11.23 percent was noticed by 'yarn spun from silk waste' (HS 5005), while the lowest growth rate of –10.56 percent has been experienced by 'silkworm cocoons' (HS 5001). As compared to sub-period-I, the exports of all the seven commodities decreased during sub-period-II, thus holding poor prospects for the future, and hence, this can be concluded that the commodities of this group do not meet the requirements of international customers. Sincere efforts should be made in this context, and research must be done by the exporting firms to examine the changing needs and preferences of the customers in the international market.

Wool, fine or coarse animal hair, horsehair yarn and woven fabric (HS 51) product group

During the whole period, seven products experienced growth rates higher than the growth rate of the group (7.06 percent). The highest growth rate of 24.41 percent has been experienced by 'Wool & animal hair carded and combed' (HS 5105), followed by 'Waste of wool or of animal hair' (18.91 percent) (HS 5103),'Woven fabrics of coarse animal hair' (HS 5113) (16.63 percent),'Yarn of carded wool' (14.70 percent), 'Yarn of fine animal hair' (HS 5106) (12.34 percent), and 'Wool not carded or combed' (HS 5101) (8.67 percent), while a negative growth rate of –6.89 percent and –5.55 percent was recorded in case of 'Fine or coarse animal hair not carded or combed' (HS 5102) and 'Yarn of wool or fine animal hair' (HS 5109), respectively.

As compared to sub-period-I, there was a rapid increase in the growth rate of exports of only three products, namely 'Fine or coarse animal hair not carded or combed,' 'Waste of wool or of animal hair,' and 'Yarn of combed wool.' However, there was rapid decline in the growth rate of exports of eight products, namely 'Wool not carded or combed,' 'Garneted stock of wool or animal hair,' 'Wool & animal hair carded and combed,' 'Yarn of carded wool,' 'Yarn of fine animal hair,' 'Yarn of coarse animal hair,' 'Woven fabrics of combed wool,' and 'Woven fabrics of coarse animal hair,' due to inadequate and outdated processing facilities for growers of specialty fibres, which affects the quality of the products, and also due to a fall in global demand for woollen products, indicating their poor export performance.

Cotton (HS Code 52) product group

During the whole period, five products experienced growth rates higher than the group (8.68 percent). The highest growth rate of 22.71 percent has been experienced by 'cotton, not carded or combed,' while the lowest growth rate of 2.01 percent was recorded (HS 5211). The negative growth rate of exports has been experienced by 'Cotton yarn (not sewing thread) retail packed' (HS 5207) (–11.62 percent) and 'Woven fabrics of cotton, containing less than 85% by weight of cotton, mixed mainly or solely with manmade fibres, weighing more than 200 g/m2' (HS 5210) (–4.12 percent).

A comparative analysis of the two sub-periods reveals that six products, namely 'Cotton, not carded or combed' (HS 5201), 'Cotton waste' (HS 5202), 'Cotton yarn (other than sewing thread), containing 85% or more by weight of cotton, not put up for retail sale' (HS 5205), 'Woven fabrics of cotton, containing 85% or more by weight of cotton, weighing not more than 200 g/m2' (HS 5208), 'Woven fabrics of cotton, containing less than 85% by weight of cotton, mixed mainly or solely with manmade fibres, weighing more than 200 g/m2' (HS 5211), and 'Other woven fabrics of cotton' (HS 5212), experienced rapid increase in growth rate of exports during the 2003–2015 sub-period as compared to the 1991–2002 sub-period, whereas six products (HS 5203, HS 5204, HS 5206, HS 5207, HS 5209, and HS 5210) experienced a decrease in growth rate of exports during sub-period-II. This may be due to a decline in the EC as a result of cotton contamination. However, CAGR in sub-period-II improved from 6.42 percent in sub-period-I to 14.02 percent in sub-period-II.

Vegetable textile fibres, paper yarn & woven fabric of paper yarn (HS 53) product group

During the whole period, seven products experienced growth rates higher than the group (6.20%). The highest growth rate of 36.27 percent has been experienced by 'Coconut, abacca, ramie etc.' (HS 5305), followed by 'Woven fabrics of flax' (HS 5309) (34.85%), 'Flax, raw etc. but not spun' (HS 5301) (27.94%), and 'Woven fabrics of vegetable textile fibers' (HS 5311) (21.64%). A negative growth rate has been experienced by 'Sisal & other agave textile fibers' (HS 5304) (–15.45%) and 'yarn of vegetable textile fibers' (HS 5308) with 0.94 percent.

Manmade filaments; strip and the like of manmade textile materials (HS 54) product group

During the whole period, three products experienced growth rates higher than the group (11.86%). The highest growth rate of 20.07 percent has been experienced by 'Synthetic monofilament' (HS 5404), followed by 'Synthetic filament yarn' (HS 5402) (17.02%) and 'Woven fabrics of synthetic filament yarn, including woven fabrics obtained from materials of heading 5404' (HS 5407) (12.11%). The lowest growth rate of 2.71 percent was recorded in case of 'Artificial filament yarn' (HS 5403). Three products, namely 'Art monofilament of 67 decitex or more' (HS 5405) (–2.67%), 'Manmade filament yarn' (HS 5406) (–2.27%), and 'Woven fabric of artificial filament yarn' (HS 5408) (–1.88%), experienced a negative growth rate of exports during this period.

Man-made staple fibres (HS 55) product group

During the whole period, six products experienced growth rates higher than the group (13.42%). The highest growth rate of 27.09 percent has been experienced by HS 5504, while the lowest growth rate of 0.49 percent was recorded in case of 'Synthetic staple fibers, carded, combed' (HS 5506). A negative growth rate (–8.43%) was experienced by HS 5507. As compared to sub-period-I, only six products experienced an increase in growth rate of exports during sub-period-II. On the other hand, ten products experienced a decline in growth rate of exports during sub-period-II, indicating the poor export performance of these products.

Wadding, felt & nonwovens, special yarns, twine, cordage, ropes, cables & articles (HS 56) product group

The findings reveal that during the whole period, four products noticed growth rates higher than the group (16.60%). The highest growth rate of 41.04 percent has been experienced by 'Nonwovens, whether or not impregnated etc.' (HS 5603), followed by 'Knotted net of twine etc., fish net' (HS 5608) (23.70%), while the lowest growth rate of 9.20 percent was recorded in case of 'Rub thread & corded, textile covering, textile yarn' (HS 5604). As compared to sub-period-I, sub-period-II witnessed an increase in growth rate of exports in case of three products (rapid increase in case of 'nonwovens, whether or not impregnated etc.'). There has been a decline in growth rate of exports in case of six products.

Carpets and other textile floor coverings (HS 57) product group

It can be concluded that during the whole period, the highest growth rate of 31.47 percent has been experienced by HS 5704. As compared to sub-period-I, sub-period-II witnessed an increase in growth rate of exports in case of four products. Only one commodity out of five registered decline in the export growth from 23.41 percent in 1991–2002 to 17.31 percent in 2003–2015, i.e. 'carpets & other textile floor coverings, tufted.'

Fabrics; special woven or tufted fabric, lace, tapestries, embroidery (HS 58) product group

During the whole period, the highest growth rate of 21.56 percent has been experienced by 'Narrow woven fabrics,' followed by 'Embroidery in the piece, in strips' (12.11%), while the lowest growth rate of 2.97 percent was recorded in case of 'Hand-woven tapestries,' and negative growth was experienced by only 1 commodity out of 11, i.e. 'Woven terry fabrics' (−1.41%). In comparison to sub-period-I, only two products, namely 'Tulles & other net fabrics,' and 'Hand-woven tapestries,' experienced increase in growth rate of exports, while nine products experienced a decline in growth rate of exports, indicating the poor performance of these products.

Impregnated, coated, covered or laminated textile products (HS code 59) product group

The examination during the whole period points out that the highest growth rate of 23.55 percent has been experienced by 'Rubberized textile fabrics,' followed by 'Textile book covered fabric' (19.32%) and 'Textile wall coverings' (18.72%), while the lowest growth rate of 5.32 percent was recorded in case of 'Textile hose piping and similar textile tubing.' As compared to sub-period-I, four products experienced an increase in growth rate of exports during sub-period-II. The products were 'Textile book covered fabric,' 'Textile fabrics coat etc.,' 'Textile wicks for lamps etc. and gas mantles,' and 'Textile hose piping and similar textile,' but maximum decline was in case of 'textile wall coverings' (growth rate decreased from 45.42% to –1.48%).

Knitted or crocheted fabrics (HS Code 60) product group

The examination during sub-period-I reveals that the lower growth rate was the result of the negative growth rate of –10.64 percent experienced by 'Knitted or crocheted fabrics of a width not exceeding 30 cm, containing by weight 5% or more of elastomeric yarn or rubber thread' (HS 6002). This commodity once again showed depressing performance in 2003–2015 (–4.01%). During the whole period, i.e. 1991–2015, 'Pile fabrics incl. long pile fabrics and terry fabrics, knitted or crocheted' showed positive growth (7.6%), and 'Knitted/crocheted fabrics' export growth was poor during the whole period (–11.39%).

Apparel and clothing accessories, knitted or crocheted (HS 61) product group

During the whole period, the highest growth rate of 22.01 percent has been experienced by 'Other garments, knitted or crocheted' (HS 6114), followed by 'Babies' garments & accessories' (HS 6111) (19.55%), 'Gloves, mittens & mitts' (HS 6116) (18.57%), and 'T-shirts, singlets and other vests, knitted or crocheted' (HS 6109) (17.85%), while the lowest growth rate of 1.28 percent was recorded in case of 'Women's or girls' overcoats etc.' (HS 6102). In comparison to the pre-WTO sub-period, only four products experienced an increase in growth rate of exports during the 2003–2015 sub-period, and the rest of 13 products registered negative growth in the 2003–2015 sub-period.

Apparel and clothing accessories, not knitted or crocheted (HS 62) product group

During the whole period, seven products experienced growth rates higher than the group (7.11 percent). The highest growth rate of 25.68 percent has been experienced by 'bras, girdles, garters etc.,' while the lowest growth rate (0.5%) was recorded in case of 'Women's or girls' overcoats etc.' Most of the products (nine products) experienced decrease in growth rate of exports during the 2003–2015 sub-period as compared to the 1991–2002 sub-period.

Maximum decline in growth rate has been experienced by 'women's or girls' slips,' from 24.51% during sub-period-I to –12.91% during sub-period-II.

Textiles, made up articles; sets; worn clothing & worn textile articles (HS 63) product group

During the whole period, six products experienced growth rates higher than the growth rate of the group (11.70%). The highest growth rate of 47.32 percent has been experienced by 'Worn clothing & other worn textile articles,' followed by 'Bed linen, table linen, toilet linen (30.51%), while the lowest growth rate (8.18%) was recorded in case of 'Furnishing articles of textile materials.' As compared to sub-period-I, only one product experienced an increase in growth rate of exports during sub-period-II, i.e. 'Furnishing articles of textile materials,' from –2.35 percent to 22.26 percent. The one major reason for the decline in exports of some of the textile commodities is the use of outdated machinery in the processing segment, resulting in inadequate quality of the finished products. Another reason for the fall in global demand for woollen products is sluggish market conditions. The decline in the growth rate of exports of raw silk is due to the poor quality of the raw silk, which did not meet requirements of world markets.

Direction of India's textile exports

It is very important to identify the direction of trade as it reflects the export destinations and also highlight the addition of new export markets in the world market. An analysis of the direction of India's textile exports reveals that in 1995, the highest share of 23.29 percent of India's textile exports was directed to the U.S., followed by Germany (11.12 percent) and the UK (10.37 percent). In 2005, the U.S. once again accounted for the highest share of 29.80 percent, followed by the UK (8.62 percent), Germany (7.19 percent), and the UAE (6.28 percent). The share of the former USSR decreased from 2.30 percent in 1995 to 0.88 percent in 2005, probably because of the disintegration of the former USSR in 1991, while other countries experienced relatively small variations in shares, which remained almost at the same level. The U.S. still remained the major market for exports in the year 2015 with the highest share of 19.08 percent. However, the share declined in comparison to 1995 and 2005, followed by the UAE (9.84 percent share), the UK (6.96 percent), Sri Lanka (5.36 percent share), and Germany (4.39 percent), which indicates addition of more export destinations for Indian textile exports.

Besides the UK, Germany, Japan, China HK SAR, the Netherlands, Switzerland, Mauritius, Austria, Switzerland, and Singapore lost importance in India's textile exports, while the UAE, Italy, Sri Lanka, Saudi Arabia, Turkey, China, and Egypt gained importance in exports. This reveals that Indian textile commodities have been able to acquire new export markets in the global market. Hence it can be concluded that India's textile exports are diversified to a number of international markets in the post-reform period. This means that the textile commodities of India have established their presence in the international markets.

Determinants of export competitiveness

The select determinants are found to have different relationships with EC for the textile industry and its two groups. The findings of the Granger causality test show the presence of only uni-directional causality for all the variables in case of textile industry running from LP, CP, unit labour cost (ULC), ER, and REER to EC. These results are also in line with the earlier studies conducted by De Grauwe and Verfaille (1988), Broll and Eckwert (1999). The results show the absence of feedback effects. However, feedback effects or bi-directional relationship of ULC with EC is found in case of the 'Textiles' group and only uni-directional causality running from LP and ER to EC, which indicates that the selected variables have effects on the EC of the 'Textiles' group. However, no causality is found running from CP and REER to EC. These findings support the study conducted by Ito and Shimizu, 2015. In case of the 'Textile Products' group, the findings of the Granger causality test show the presence of only uni-directional causality running from LP, CP, ULC, and ER to EC, which indicates that the selected variables have effects on the EC of the 'Textiles' group. However, no causality is found running from REER to EC. These findings support the work of Jian (2007).

The findings of the Johansen and Juselius co-integration test reveal the long-run relationship between the select variables for the Indian textile industry and its two groups, 'Textiles' and 'Textile Products.' However, the number of co-integrating equations is different for each group. The trace statistics have six co-integrating equations at 5 percent level, and maximum Eigen value statistics have four co-integrated equations for the textile industry in the model. These findings are supported by Grossman and Helpman (1991); Rivera-Batiz and Romer (1991). The trace statistics and maximum Eigen value have five co-integrated equations in the model for the 'Textiles' group. However, in case of the 'Textile Products' group, there are three co-integrating equations, and maximum Eigen value statistics have one co-integrated equation in the model.

The regression model also highlights that the values of R-squared and adjusted R-squared are high for the textile industry and its two groups. In case of the textile industry, the values of R-squared and adjusted R-squared are 0.840 and 0.795, respectively, for the 'Textiles' group 0.848 and 0.806, respectively, and 0.694 and 0.609, respectively, for the 'Textile Products' group. The corresponding p-values are also found to be significant, which indicates that all the variables such as LP, CP, ULC, ER, and REER have a significant influence on the EC. However, this impact of independent variables (IVs) on dependent variables (IVs) is lower for the 'Textile Products' group as compared to that of the textile industry and 'Textiles' group. These findings support the studies of Cheung and Sengupta, 2013; Kathuria, 2013).

The results of the VECM to examine the long-run coefficient of the co-integrating model reveal that there is no long-run causality running from IVs, i.e. LP, CP, ULC, ER, and REER to the DV, i.e. EC in case of the textile industry. However, there is the presence of long-run causality running from IV to DV in case of the 'Textiles' group and the 'Textile Products' group. These findings also support Fang, Lai, and Miller (2004). A Wald test to check the short-run causality presents that there is no short-run causality running from IVs to DV in case of the textile industry. However, the findings for the 'Textiles' group and the 'Textile Products' group present a contradictory picture and reveals the presence of short-run causality running from IVs to DV. In case of the 'Textiles' group, there is short-run causality running from CP and ULC to EC. These findings also support Ito and Shimizu (2015). However, for LP, ER, and REER there is no short-run causality found, as *p*-values are non-significant at a 5 percent level of significance. This finding is also supported by Gotur (1985) and Koray and Lastrapes (1989). In case of the 'Textile Products' group, there is short-run causality running from ULC and ER to EC. These findings are in line with Biselli (2009); Jaussaud and Rey (2012); Zia and Mahmood (2013). However, for LP, CP, and REER there is no short-run causality running from LP, CP, and REER to EC, as *p*-values are non-significant at a 5 percent level of significance.

The results of the diagnostic test for the VECM suggest that the model is normally distributed, and the model also does not suffer from the problems of serial correlation and heteroskedasticity. So it can be concluded that all the models have the property of goodness of fit for the textile industry and its two groups, i.e. 'Textiles' group and 'Textile Products' group. So it can be concluded that in addition to cheap labour cost, a thriving domestic market is the opportunity that lies ahead of the industry. The abolition of the quota in the post-reform era can be regarded as an opportunity and a threat, an opportunity since the marketplace will no longer be limited and a threat as markets will no longer be assured by quotas, and even the home marketplace will be free to competition. The exporting firms need to make sure the use of advanced technology to be more competitive in the international market so that export performance can improve. There is need to examine the declining trends in the export growth performance of HS 5001, HS 5002, HS 5102, HS 5109, HS 5207, HS 5210, HS 5304, HS 5405, HS 5406, HS 5507, HS 5802, HS 5904, and HS 6002. Apart from this, the firms should make sure that the various factors such as labour and CP, ULC, ER, and REER impact the EC and all these variables move together in the long run.

Major recommendations

The inception of economic reforms of liberalization and globalization within the country has posed new challenges and opportunities for the Indian textile industry. There is an urgent need for improvement in productivity and hence competitiveness of this industry. The study of growth performance and trends in labour and CP in the Indian textile industry and its groups presented to some extent a pessimistic representation of the Indian textile industry. This is largely due to decreasing growth rate of labour and CP in the 'Textile Products' group, which is a serious concern because the global market is becoming more and more competitive and hence requiring high productivity to sustain in the international markets.

Improvement in productivity indicates the realization of more output from the same inputs or, alternatively, using lesser inputs to achieve the same output. The growth in the productivity trends is needed not only to increase output but also to improve the competitiveness in the domestic and international markets. So there is a need to upgrade the technology level in the textile firms. This can be achieved by encouraging the textile firms to make the most of the larger funds available under the Technology Upgradation Fund Scheme (TUFS). TUFS offers loans to the industry at a lower rate of interest to upgrade the existing technology. It is suggested to the Apparel Export Promotion Council of India to regularly organize awareness camps for textile firms to make them conscious about the various government policies. Even in the 'Textiles' group, there is need to strengthen the technological advancements, as this sector is still plagued with out-dated technology. So the textile firms have to focus on the transfer of technology so that the obsolete technology may be replaced with the advanced ones and hence the productivity may increase.

In order to improve the LP in the 'Textile Products' group, there is need of labour reforms that encourage them to achieve the desired level of LP. Productivity-based wage policies should be implemented by textile firms. The performance management system in the textile firms should be implemented in such a way that captures the development inputs for labour. Further, training and development needs can be designed on the basis of the captured development inputs for each employee. This possibly can be one measure for improvement in the LP.

An examination of employment elasticities reveals that 'Textile Products' group has more employment potential, so bringing into play the advanced technology may possibly lead to retrenchment of labour in this group. So it is recommended to make use of intermediate technology for this group.

Further, there is need to examine the declining trends in the export growth performance of 'silkworm cocoons' (HS 5001), 'raw silk' (HS 5002), 'Fine or coarse animal hair not carded or combed' (HS 5102), 'Yarn of wool or fine animal hair' (HS 5109), 'Cotton yarn (not sewing thread) retail packed'

(HS 5207), 'Woven cotton fabrics, un 85% cot, mmf mix, n/ov 200 g/m2' (HS 5210), 'Sisal & other agave text fibers' (HS 5304), 'Art monof, n/un 67 dec crs n/ov 1mm' (HS 5405), 'Manmade filament yarn' (HS 5406), 'Artificial staple fiber crd cmd' (HS 5507), 'Woven terry fabrics' (HS 5802), 'Linoleum, floor cover with coat etc. on a text base' (HS 5904), and 'Knitted/crocheted fabrics' (HS 6002). There is a need to take the measures for the declining trend in these products in the post-reform regime. One possible measure can be strengthening of research and development efforts. Another measure can be bridging the gap between demand and supply in terms of both quality and quantity, which would help in increasing textile and clothing exports. In addition to this, the role of the government is also crucial. The government support and incentives are the need of the hour to encourage the domestic production of fibres to make sure adequate supply of fibres to the industry over the long term. To improve apparel exports, there is need to enter into regional trade agreements with trading partners like the North American Free Trade Agreement, which allows free trade among Mexico, the U.S., and Canada. The cotton sector can be strengthened through an upgraded and reformed marketing system and through conscious branding of cotton for use. There is need to evolve a strategy that aims at faster product innovation and quick responses to the changing tastes and preferences to excel in garment exports.

CP, ULC, and ER came out as significant determinants of EC in case of the 'Textiles' and 'Textile Products' groups. The obsolete technology needs to be replaced with the modern one, and for this purpose, the textile firms have to invest in the technology. The firms are advised to make the most of the larger funds available under TUFS. The firms are also advised to minimize labour costs to gain the competitiveness in the world markets. But this practice needs to be wisely formulated, as at times, the firms may follow an unsustainable path of cost-cutting strategies to join the global value chain. This will make the conditions worse for millions of workers engaged in the textile sector. Depreciation in the rupee can make the exports cheaper in the world market and increase the demand for exported goods, but this has a limited scope, as it will also increase the cost of imported inputs. In addition to policy implications, this volume possesses academic and practical implications. The researchers in this field would get comprehensive insights about the various determinants of EC and export performance of the Indian textile industry, especially at the disaggregate level. Moreover, the textile exporters would be in a better position to identify the major trading partners and new export markets in the world market.

References

Bedi, S. J., and Cororaton, C. B. (2008). *Cotton-textile-apparel sectors of India situations and challenges faced markets*. The International Food Policy Research Institute, Discussion Paper, 801.

Biselli, M. (2009). *China's role in the global textile industry*. China Europe International Business School, Student Research Projects/Outputs, 39.

Broll, U., and Eckwert, B. (1999). Exchange rate volatility and international trade. *Southern Economic Journal*, 66, 178–185.

Cheung, Y. W., and Sengupta, S. (2013). Impact of exchange rate movements on exports: An analysis of Indian non-financial sector firms. *Journal of International Money and Finance*, 39, 231–245.

De Grauwe, P., and Verfaille, G. (1988). Exchange rate variability, misalignment, and the European monetary system. In *Misalignment of exchange rates: Effects on trade and industry* (pp. 77–104). Chicago: University of Chicago Press.

Fang, W., Lai, Y., and Miller, S. (2004). *Export promotion through exchange rate policy: Exchange rate depreciation or stabilization?* Department of Economics, University of Connecticut, Working Papers, 2005–2007.

Gotur, P. (1985). Effects of exchange rate volatility on trade: Some further evidence. *Staff Papers*, 32(3), 475–512.

Grossman, G., and Helpman, E. (1991). *Innovation and growth in the global economy*. Cambridge: MIT Press.

Ito, K., and Shimizu, J. (2015). Industry-level competitiveness, productivity and effective exchange rates in East Asia. *Asian Economic Journal*, 29(2), 181–214.

Jaussaud, J., and Rey, S. (2012). Long-run determinants Japanese export to China and the United States: A sectoral analysis. *Pacific Economic Review*, 17(1), 1–28.

Jian, L. Ü. (2007). Empirical study on the influence of RMB exchange rate misalignment on China's export. *Frontiers of Economics in China*, 2(2), 224–236.

Kathuria, M. L. (2013). Analyzing competitiveness of clothing export sector of India and Bangladesh: Dynamic revealed comparative advantage approach. *Competitiveness Review: An International Business Journal*, 23(2), 131–157.

Koray, F., and Lastrapes, W. D. (1989). Real exchange rate volatility and US bilateral trade: A VAR approach. *Review of Economics and Statistics*, 71(4), 708–712.

Rivera-Batiz, L. A., and Romer, P. (1991). Economic integration and endogenous growth. *The Quarterly Journal of Economics*, 106(2), 531–555.

USITC. (2001). *Annual report*. Washington, DC: USITC.

Zia, U., and Mahmood, Z. (2013). Exchange rate depreciation and export price competitiveness: The case of Pakistani manufacturing industries. *Journal of the Asia Pacific Economy*, 18(4), 529–542.

Appendix 1
Commodity classification

Appendix 1.1 Commodity Classification of HS 50 at Four-Digit Level

Sr. No.	HS Code	Products
1	5001	Silkworm cocoons suitable for reeling
2	5002	Raw silk (not thrown)
3	5003	Silk waste (including cocoons unsuitable for reeling, yarn waste and garneted stock)
4	5004	Silk yarn (other than yarn spun from silk waste) not put up for retail sale
5	5005	Yarn spun from silk waste, not put up for retail sale
6	5006	Silk yarn and yarn spun from silk waste, put up for retail sale; silk-worm gut
7	5007	Woven fabrics of silk or of silk waste

Appendix 1.2 Commodity Classification of HS 51 at Four-Digit Level

Sr. No.	HS Code	Products
1	5101	Wool not carded or combed
2	5102	Fine or coarse animal hair not carded or combed
3	5103	Waste of wool or of animal hair, including yarn waste but excluding garnetted stock
4	5104	Garnetted stock of wool or of fine or coarse animal hair
5	5105	Wool and fine or coarse animal hair, carded or combed (including combed wool in fragments)
6	5106	Yarn of carded wool, not put up for retail sale
7	5107	Yarn of combed wool, not put up for retail sale
8	5108	Yarn of fine animal hair (carded or combed), not put up for retail sale
9	5109	Yarn of wool or fine animal hair, put up for retail sale
10	5110	Yarn of coarse animal hair or of horse hair (including gimped horsehair yarn), whether or not put up for retail sale
11	5111	Woven fabrics of carded wool or of carded fine animal hair
12	5112	Woven fabrics of combed wool or of combed fine animal hair
13	5113	Woven fabrics of coarse animal hair or of horse hair

Appendix 1.3 Commodity Classification of HS 52 at Four-Digit Level

Sr. No.	HS Code	Products
1	5201	Cotton, not carded or combed
2	5202	Cotton waste (including yarn waste and garnetted stock)
3	5203	Cotton, carded or combed
4	5204	Cotton sewing thread, whether or not put up for retail sale
5	5205	Cotton yarn (other than sewing thread), containing 85% or more by weight of cotton, not put up for retail sale
6	5206	Cotton yarn (other than sewing thread), containing less than 85% by weight of cotton, not put up for retail sale
7	5207	Cotton yarn (other than sewing thread) put up for retail sale
8	5208	Woven fabrics of cotton, containing 85% or more by weight of cotton, weighing not more than 200 g/m^2
9	5209	Woven fabrics of cotton, containing 85% or more by weight of cotton, weighing more than 200 g/m^2
10	5210	Woven fabrics of cotton, containing less than 85% by weight of cotton, mixed mainly or solely with manmade fibres, weighing not more than 200 g/m^2
11	5211	Woven fabrics of cotton, containing less than 85% by weight of cotton, mixed mainly or solely with manmade fibres, weighing more than 200 g/m^2
12	5212	Other woven fabrics of cotton

Appendix 1.4 Commodity Classification of HS 53 at Four-Digit Level

Sr. No.	HS Code	Products
1	5301	Flax, raw or processed but not spun; flax tow and waste (including yarn waste and garnetted stock)
2	5302	True hemp (cannabis sativa l), raw or processed but not spun; tow and waste of true hemp (including yarn waste and garnetted stock)
3	5303	Jute and other textile bast fibres (excluding flax, true hemp and ramie), raw or processed but not spun; tow and waste of these fibres (including yarn waste and garnetted stock)
4	5304	Sisal & other agave textile fibers
5	5305	Coconut, abaca (manila hemp or musa textilis nee), ramie and other vegetable textile fibres, not elsewhere specified or included, raw or processed but not spun; tow, noils and waste of these fibres (including yarn waste and garnetted stock)
6	5306	Flax yarn
7	5307	Yarn of jute or of other textile bast fibres of heading 5303
8	5308	Yarn of other vegetable textile fibres; paper yarn
9	5309	Woven fabrics of flax
10	5310	Woven fabrics of jute or of other textile base fibres of heading 5303
11	5311	Woven fabrics of other vegetable textile fibres; woven fabrics of paper yarn

Appendix 1.5 Commodity Classification of HS 54 at Four-Digit Level

Sr. No.	HS Code	Products
1	5401	Sewing thread of man-made filaments, whether or not put up for retail sale
2	5402	Synthetic filament yarn (other than sewing thread), not put up for retail sale, including synthetic monofilament of less than 67 decitex
3	5403	Artificial filament yarn (other than sewing thread), not put for retail sale, including artificial mono filament of less than 67 decitex
4	5404	Synthetic monofilament of 67 decitex or more and of which no cross-sectional dimension exceeds 1 mm; strip and the like (for example, artificial straw) of synthetic textile materials of an apparent width not exceeding 5 mm
5	5405	Art monofilament of 67 decitex or more
6	5406	Manmade filament yarn
7	5407	Woven fabrics of synthetic filament yarn, including woven fabrics obtained from materials of heading 5404
8	5408	Woven fabrics of artificial filament yarn, including woven fabrics obtained from materials of heading 5405

Appendix 1.6 Commodity Classification of HS 55 at Four-Digit Level

Sr. No	HS Code	Products
1	5501	Wool, not carded or combed
2	5502	Artificial filament tow
3	5503	Synthetic staple fibres, not carded, combed or otherwise processed for spinning
4	5504	Artificial staple fibres, not carded, combed or otherwise processed for spinning
5	5505	Waste (including noils, yarn waste and garnetted stock) of man-made fibres
6	5506	Synthetic staple fibres, carded combed or otherwise processed for spinning
7	5507	Artificial staple fibres, carded, combed or otherwise processed for spinning
8	5508	Sewing thread of man-made staple fibres, whether or not put up for retail sale
9	5509	Yarn (other than sewing thread) of synthetic staple fibres, not put up for retail sale
10	5510	Yarn (other than sewing thread) of artificial staple fibres, not put up for retail sale
11	5511	Yarn (other than sewing thread) of man-made staple fibres, put up for retail sale

(*Continued*)

Appendix 1.6 (Continued)

Sr. No	HS Code	Products
12	5512	Woven fabrics of synthetic staple fibres, containing 85% or more by weight of synthetic staple fibres
13	5513	Woven fabrics of synthetic staple fibres, containing less than 85% by weight of such fibres, mixed mainly or solely with cotton, of a weight not exceeding 170 g/m^2
14	5514	Woven fabrics of synthetic staple fibres, containing less than 85% by weight of such fibres, mixed mainly or solely with cotton, of a weight exceeding 170 g/m^2
15	5515	Other woven fabrics of synthetic staple fibres
16	5516	Woven fabrics of artificial staple fibres

Appendix 1.7 Commodity Classification of HS 56 at Four-Digit Level

Sr. No.	HS Code	Products
1	5601	Wadding of textile materials and articles thereof; textile fibres, not exceeding 5 mm in length (flock), textile dust and mill neps
2	5602	Felt, whether or not impregnated, coated, covered or laminated
3	5603	Nonwovens, whether or not impregnated, coated, covered or laminated.
4	5604	Rubber thread & cord, textile covered; textile yarn, and strip and the like of heading 5404 or 5405, impregnated, coated, covered or sheathed with rubber or plastics
5	5605	Metallised yarn, whether or not gimped being textile yarn, or strip or the like of heading 5404 or 5405, combined with metal in the form of thread, strip or powder or covered with metal
6	5606	Gimped yarn, and strip and the like of heading 5404 or 5405, gimped (other than those of heading 5605 and gimped horsehair yarn); chenille yarn (including flock chenille yarn); loop wale-yarn
7	5607	Twine, cordage, ropes and cables, whether or not plaited or braided and whether or not impregnated, coated, covered or sheathed with rubber or plastics
8	5608	Knotted netting of twine, cordage or rope; made up fishing nets and other made up nets, of textile materials
9	5609	Articles of yarn, strip or the like of heading 5404 or 5405, twine, cordage, rope or cables, not elsewhere specified or included

Appendix 1.8 Commodity Classification of HS 57 at Four-Digit Level

Sr. No.	HS Code	Products
1	5701	Carpets and other textile floor coverings, knotted, whether or not made
2	5702	Carpets and other textile floor coverings, woven, not tufted or flocked, whether or not made up, including "kelem", "schumacks", "karamanie" and similar hand-woven rugs
3	5703	Carpets and other textile floor coverings, tufted, whether or not made up
4	5704	Carpets and other textile floor coverings, of felt, not tufted or flocked, whether or not made up
5	5705	Other carpets and other textile floor coverings, whether or not made up

Appendix 1.9 Commodity Classification of HS 58 at Four-Digit Level

Sr. No.	HS Code	Products
1	5801	Woven pile fabrics and chenille fabrics, other than fabrics of heading 5802 or 5806
2	5802	Terry towelling and similar woven terry fabrics, other than narrow fabrics of heading 5806; tufted textile fabrics, other than products of heading 5703
3	5803	Gauze other than narrow fabrics of heading 5806
4	5804	Tulles and other net fabrics, not including woven, knitted or crocheted fabrics; lace in the piece, in strips or in motifs, other than fabrics of heading 6002 to 6006
5	5805	Hand-woven tapestries of the type gobelins, flanders, aubusson, beauvais and the like, and needle-worked tapestries (for example, petit point, cross stitch), whether or not made up
6	5806	Narrow woven fabrics other than goods of heading 5807; narrow fabrics consisting of warp without weft assembled by means of an adhesive (bolducs)
7	5807	Labels, badges and similar articles of textile materials, in the piece, in strips or cut to shape or size not embroidered
8	5808	Braids in the piece; ornamental trimmings in the piece, without embroidery, other than knitted or crocheted; tassels, pompons and similar articles
9	5809	Woven fabrics of metal thread and woven fabrics of metallised yarn of heading 5605, of a kind used in apparel, as furnishing fabrics or for similar purposes, not elsewhere specified or included
10	5810	Embroidery in the piece, in strips or in motifs
11	5811	Quilted textile products in the piece, composed of one or more layers of textile materials assembled with padding by stitching or otherwise, other than embroidery of heading 5810

Appendix 1.10 Commodity Classification of HS 59 at Four-Digit Level

Sr. No.	HS Code	Products
1	5901	Textile fabrics coated with gum or amylaceous substances, of a kind used for the outer covers of books or the like; tracing cloth; prepared painting canvas; buckram and similar stiffened textile fabrics of a kind used for hat foundations
2	5902	Tyre cord fabric of high tenacity yarn of nylon or other polyamides, polyesters or viscose rayon
3	5903	Textile fabrics, impregnated, coated, covered or laminated
4	5904	Linoleum, whether or not cut to shape; floor coverings consisting of a coating or covering applied on a textile backing, whether or not cut to shape
5	5905	Textile wall coverings
6	5906	Rubberised textile fabrics, other than those of heading 5902
7	5907	Textile fabrics otherwise impregnated, coated or covered; painted canvas being theatrical scenery, studio back-cloths or the like
8	5908	Textile wicks, woven, plaited or knitted, for lamps, stoves, lighters, candles or the like; incandescent gas mantles and tubular knitted gas mantle fabric therefor, whether or not impregnated
9	5909	Textile hose piping and similar textile tubing, with or without lining, armour or accessories of other materials
10	5910	Transmission or conveyor belts or belting, of textile material, whether or not impregnated, coated, covered or laminated with plastics, or reinforced with metal or other material
11	5911	Textile products and articles, for technical uses, specified in note 7 to this chapter

Appendix 1.11 Commodity Classification of HS 60 at Four-Digit Level

Sr. No.	HS Code	Products
1	6001	Pile fabrics, including long pile fabrics and terry fabrics, knitted or crocheted
2	6002	Knitted or crocheted fabrics of a width not exceeding 30 cm, containing by weight 5% or more of elastomeric yarn or rubber thread, other than

Appendix 1.12 Commodity Classification of HS 61 at Four-Digit Level

Sr. No.	HS Code	Products
1	6101	Men's or boys' overcoats, carcoats, capes, cloaks, anoraks (including skijackets), wind-cheaters, windjackets and similar articles, knitted or crocheted, other than those of heading 6103
2	6102	Women's or girls' overcoats, carcoats, capes, cloaks, anoraks (including skijackets), wind-cheaters, windjackets and similar articles, knitted or crocheted, other than those of heading 6104
3	6103	Men's or boys' suits, ensembles, jackets, blazers, trousers, bib and brace overalls, breeches and shorts (other than swim wear), knitted or crocheted
4	6104	Women's or girls' suits, ensembles, jackets, blazers, dresses, skirts, divided skirts, trousers, bib and brace overalls, breeches and shorts (other than swim wear), knitted or crocheted
5	6105	Men's or boys' shirts, knitted or crocheted
6	6106	Women's or girls' blouses, shirts and shirt-blouses, knitted or crocheted
7	6107	Men's or boys' underpants, briefs, nightshirts, pyjamas, bathrobes, dressing gowns and similar articles, knitted or crocheted
8	6108	Women's or girls' slips, petticoats, briefs, panties, night dresses, pyjamas, negligees, bathrobes, dressing gowns and similar articles, knitted or crocheted
9	6109	T-shirts, singlets and other vests, knitted or crocheted
10	6110	Jerseys, pullovers, cardigans, waistcoats and similar articles, knitted or crocheted
11	6111	Babies' garments and clothing accessories, knitted or crocheted
12	6112	Track suits, ski suits and swimwear, knitted or crocheted
13	6113	Garments, knit etc., coated et
14	6114	Other garments, knitted or crocheted
15	6115	Pantyhose, tights, stockings, socks and other hosiery, including graduated compression hosiery (for example, stockings for varicose veins) and footwear without applied soles, knitted or crocheted
16	6116	Gloves, mittens and mitts, knitted or crocheted
17	6117	Other made up clothing accessories, knitted or crocheted; knitted or crocheted parts of garment.

Appendix 1.13 Commodity Classification of HS 62 at Four-Digit Level

Sr. No.	HS Code	Products
1	6201	Men's or boys' overcoats, carcoats, cloaks, anoraks (including ski-jackets), windcheaters, wind jackets and similar articles other than those of heading 6203
2	6202	Women's or girls' overcoats, car-coats, capes, cloaks, anoraks (including ski-jackets), wind-cheaters, wind-jackets and similar articles, other than those of heading 6204.
3	6203	Men's or boys' suits, ensembles, jackets, blazers, trousers bib and brace overalls, breeches and shorts (other than swimwear)
4	6204	Women's or girls' suits, ensembles, jackets, blazers, dresses, skirts, divided skirts, trousers, bib and brace overalls, breeches and shorts (other than swimwear)
5	6205	Men's or boys' shirts
6	6206	Women's or girls' blouses, shirts and shirt-blouses
7	6207	Men's or boys' singlets and other vests, underpants, briefs, nightshirts, pyjamas, bathrobes, dressing gowns and similar articles
8	6208	Women's or girls' singlets and other vests, slips, petticoats, briefs, panties, nightdresses, pyjamas, negliges, bathrobes, dressing gowns and similar articles
9	6209	Babies' garments and clothing accessories
10	6210	Garments, made up of fabrics of heading 5602, 5603, 5903, 5906 or 5907
11	6211	Track suits, ski suits and swimwear; other garments
12	6212	Brassieres, girdles, corsets, braces, suspenders, garters and similar articles and parts thereof, whether or not knitted or crocheted
13	6213	Handkerchiefs
14	6214	Shawls, scarves, mufflers, mantillas, veils and the like
15	6215	Ties, bow ties and cravats
16	6216	Gloves, mittens & mitts
17	6217	Other made up clothing accessories; parts of garments or of clothing accessories, other than those of heading 6212

Appendix 1.14 Commodity Classification of HS 63 at Four-Digit Level

Sr. No	HS Code	Products
1	6301	Blankets & traveling rugs
2	6302	Bed linen, table linen, toilet Linen and kitchen linen
3	6303	Curtains (including drapes) and interior blinds: curtain or bed valances

Sr. No	HS Code	Products
4	6304	Other furnishing articles, excluding those of heading 9404
5	6305	Sacks and bags, of a kind used for the packing of goods
6	6306	Tarpaulins, awnings and sunblinds; tents; sails for boats, sailboards or landcraft; camping goods
7	6307	Other made up articles, including dress patterns
8	6308	Needlecraft sets of woven fabric & yarn
9	6309	Worn clothing & other worn textile articles
10	6310	Used or new rags, scrap twine, cordage, rope and cables and worn out articles of twine, cordage, rope or cables, of textile materials.

Index

Note: *Italicized* pages refer to figures and **bold** pages refer to tables.

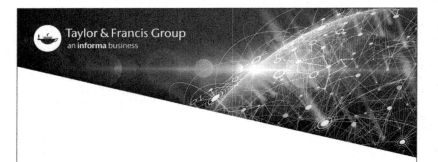

Printed in the United States
by Baker & Taylor Publisher Services